STRATEGY 3.0

FAST & FOCUSED | AGILE & ADAPTIVE

dr. stephen r. graves

Strategy 3.0
Fast & Focused | Agile & Adaptive

Organizational Strategy

dr. stephen r. graves
Strategy 3.0
Published by KJK Inc. Publishing
P.O. Box 9448
Fayetteville, AR 72702

Details in some anecdotes and stories have been changed to protect the identities of the persons involved.

ISBN 978-0-9855825-8-6

Prepared in association with Edit Resource, LLC (editresource.com)

STRATEGY 3.0
FAST & FOCUSED | AGILE & ADAPTIVE

Contents

CHAPTER 1

A LEADER AT THE CROSSROADS

CHANGE COMES TO all organizations. Leaders have the responsibility to try to look around the corner and prepare their business or nonprofit for what may lie ahead. In other words, they need to *strategize*, establishing a general plan of action for the organization based to a disconcerting degree on subjective insights and partially informed conjectures about the future.

But it's even more complicated and more fluid than that, because *strategy itself is changing*. That's what this book is about—teaching you what strategy looks like (and doesn't look like) today. What works and what no longer works.

Before we get to all that, though, it's important to remind ourselves that every strategy takes place at a crossroads in an organization's path. And standing at that crossroads is a real-live human being: a leader. Like you. And like Tom, Lane, Dev, and Jayla.

What feels familiar to you in these stories?

GO BIG OR GO HOME

Tom Chadwick told himself that he was making as much noise as a blind bear crashing through the tree branches and underbrush. He had lost the trail some time ago, but that wasn't stopping him. His goal was the summit of the mountain, and if he just kept going up, he knew he would get there eventually.

Finally he did.

Brushing himself off, he took a seat on a stone ledge and looked out over the Blue Ridge Mountains receding into the distance in every direction around him. Yet even this glorious sight could not distract him for long from the matters that had been occupying his mind.

He was staying at the lodge whose green roof was barely visible on the slope below, taking his usual "retreat before the retreat." He liked to have a day or two by himself to think before his executive team joined him for their yearly dream-a-thon for their Norfolk-based company, HomeBright Products. This year, the main topic of conversation was particularly momentous.

The company Tom had started seventeen years earlier had done well through its supply contract with a regional retailer. HomeBright's area rugs, light fixtures, accent pieces, and the like were known throughout the Mid-Atlantic states. Back at HQ, the HomeBright family was stable, prosperous, and happy—just like Tom had always wanted it to be.

The issue at hand was that their retailer was making a big push to go national, and it was pressing HomeBright to go national along with it. If Tom and his team were to agree, this raised lots of questions. They would need massive growth capital—where would it come from? Would it be possible for Tom to continue to own the majority of the company, as he had done so far? Every part of his company would feel the shock of the changes; how would the employees react? What new positions would he need to hire for? Where would they do the new manufacturing that would be required? Should he look into outsourcing customer service, or even production, to IndiAsia?

Or should he expand the company through merger instead?

Or should he try to find another retail partner that wouldn't put the external growth pressure on HomeBright?

Any one of these strategies might be the straightest avenue to success in the future. Any of them might be a route to dismal failure.

He didn't like having to make such a big decision so fast. Maybe he should just sell out and let somebody else have the headache.

Tom thought back to the excitement of founding the company when he was a young man. His wife had pointed out to him just the other day that, whenever he told stories about the company, the ones that really lit him up were the ones from the early years—when every day brought a crisis to resolve, when riches were separated from ruin by a knife's edge. Scary in the moment, exciting in retrospect. Maybe stable wasn't all it was cracked up to be.

Tom started pacing back and forth across the summit of the mountain. As he did so, he gauged the temperature of the fire in his belly for a new challenge. And he found it was pretty hot. Nah, he wouldn't sell out. Go big or go home! He still had little idea how he would take the company through the most ambitious expansion in its history. But somehow he believed that, if he kept making his own trail up and up, he'd reach the mountaintop eventually.

"ANY ONE OF THESE STRATEGIES MIGHT BE THE STRAIGHTEST AVENUE TO SUCCESS IN THE FUTURE. ANY OF THEM MIGHT BE A ROUTE TO DISMAL FAILURE."

One thing was sure: this time tomorrow, his team would be looking to him for leadership. He'd better figure out how best to provide it to them.

He paced some more.

SKINNY DOWN AND HANG ON

Lane Hutchins stuck her head in her son's bedroom doorway and said hi.

Fifteen-year-old Ryan quickly minimized the screen on his computer. The look on his face spelled guilt.

Uh-oh. Lane stepped into the room at once to investigate. Was her son viewing porn? Chatting with some nefarious character? Playing a forbidden video game?

Lane brought up the screen he'd been looking at. Amazon.

Ryan had been buying the latest in his favorite series of sports novels.

"I'm sorry, Mom," said the boy. "I know you don't like us to buy books anywhere except from a store. But it's just so much cheaper and easier, you know?"

Lane sighed. Even her own flesh and blood.

That night, as she tossed and turned as inconspicuously as she could beside her husband, she rehearsed the problems digitalization had brought to her beloved industry. Book publishing had always been an iffy enterprise, kept alive by romantics and idealists who had been born lacking the greed gene. But now, to the owner of a publishing company like herself, digitalization had introduced so many more disruptions. Was a profit-making business plan even possible anymore?

The way that online sales giants had shriveled publishing's former symbiotic partner—the brick-and-mortar bookstore—was just the beginning of it. Books themselves were going digital, and the public had shown a marked aversion for paying any price for an e-book that didn't return change from a ten-dollar bill. Worst was, you couldn't completely switch to e-books, because too many people still demanded paper books. You had to publish in, and somehow make money in, both channels—all while the total number of Americans interested in reading books of any kind or format was on a downward trend. Print-on-demand technology was *a* solution, but far from *the* solution. The conferences on the future of digital publishing that Lane had been going to had convinced her that there was no obvious solution.

Lane had to make a choice for Ripe Pickings Press, her gardening and hobby books publishing company.

For one thing, she could overcome her personal resistance to electronic publishing and choose to innovate and invest. But innovate how? Invest in what, exactly? Maybe she and her department heads could come up with a solution that would position the company splendidly for the future, but what that would look like she couldn't even guess right now.

Or she could cut costs and hope that the situation resolved itself—the get-skinny-and-hang-on approach. In other words, wait it out while letting the bigger players figure out how to thrive in the age of electronic publishing. She knew getting skinny was hardly a prescription for long-term success. But in the shorter term it might give her company a chance to survive until she saw how to master the digital intruder.

This was a more appealing option to Lane at the moment. But it left many questions in her mind. Could Ripe Pickings tread water and still hold on to customer loyalty? Which employees and which initiatives would she have to let go, and which should she retain? How lean would be lean enough? How long would they have to stay on the diet?

Lane sighed. She'd been sighing a lot lately.

And she sure wasn't sleeping.

Maybe she should slip down to the den and read something. She remembered how her best friend had raved about a new history of King Henry VIII's wives—that book sounded great. Too bad she didn't have a copy. Of course, if she ordered it on Amazon, she could get a discount and have it in two days.

She stopped herself. No, no, no!

CHANGING LANES OR A BRAND-NEW HIGHWAY

"I hope I didn't interrupt your nap," Dev Bannerjee joshed when Dave Bradshaw answered his call.

"Ha-ha. That one's always funny," Dave said. "I'll have you know, in the last twenty-four hours I attended the symphony, went scuba diving, and took a pilot's lesson." Dave—Dev's predecessor as CEO at the food processing company Greenfields—was enjoying an active retirement and Dev knew it.

"But don't worry," Dave went on. "I always have time to straighten out you wet-behind-the-ears kids." Dev had recently turned fifty-five and Dave knew it.

"Well, as long as you offer," said Dev. The two often held casual business consultations over the phone.

Dev described the company's current situation to his friend. Sales growth was continuing slow but steady, while cost-cutting measures in the last year had boosted Greenfields' cash position substantially. The company's annual planning cycle was starting up again soon, and Dev wanted to put the right options on the table.

"We've got a number of possibilities for expansion in our food offerings," Dev explained.

For example, organics continues to be a growth area. Any one of these food options is well within our competency range and would probably start yielding ROI within an acceptable time frame.

"But here's the thing I've been toying with," continued Dev. "What if we took our cash and used it to try something really different, something that's not food processing at all? Something that's got more growth potential than the food business?"

"What have you got in mind?" Dave said.

"I know it's a totally different strategy, but...real estate."

"Real estate?"

"Real estate."

"Okay, still listening."

"We've got people all over the rural parts of this country. We know where population centers are growing but where the land costs are still cheap. So what do we do? We buy raw real estate at bargain prices near these growing towns, lease it out for agriculture, then when land prices go up and developers are ready to move in, we sell off in parcels. If we do it right, the eventual markup could be steep.

"What do you think? I know it's not the usual Greenfields way. Should I even bring it up at the strategy session?"

"Let me see if I've got this right," Dave said. "You're talking about raw real estate as a new core business, not just some short-term investment for your cash?"

"Right," Dev said. "The way I'm picturing it to myself is, I'm setting out on a brand-new highway, not just making a lane change."

The older man was silent for several seconds. Then he said, "You know, Dev, people can change—I'm finding that out in my retirement. Companies can change too. I don't know if your idea is a good one or not, but if you want my advice, yeah, put it on the table."

SUNSET OR REBIRTH

In recent years, whenever Jayla Rice-Washington returned to her home country of the United States, it seemed like a foreign land to her. She had spent so much time in the East African country of Mozambique that she felt more Mozambican than American.

In 1990, when the civil war in Mozambique came to an end, Jayla—fresh out of a master's program in nonprofit management—had founded Children's Refuge Mozambique to assist in caring for the nation's vast number of orphaned boys and girls. At the outset, she and her board had defined "success" as having at least one well-run orphanage in operation under a trained Mozambican director in each of the nation's ten provinces. Before returning to the United States on this current trip, Jayla had installed a local director in remote Niassa, the last of the ten provinces her organization had reached.

Perhaps it was because of this milestone, with the resulting sense of relief and accomplishment, that Jayla felt more comfortable in returning to the United States than she had in a long time. She was in Atlanta for the annual CRM board of directors meeting.

The agenda basically came down to this: *Now what?* They had achieved "success," as originally defined, so what more—if anything—should they be doing?

Most of Jayla's board members had been with her from the beginning. She trusted them, and they trusted her, and discussions tended to be open and wide ranging.

"...NOW WHAT? THEY HAD ACHIEVED 'SUCCESS,' AS ORIGINALLY DEFINED, SO WHAT MORE—IF ANYTHING—SHOULD THEY BE DOING?"

At one point the Rev. Dr. Jeffers said, "We achieved what we wanted to. Mozambique is in a better place than it was back when we started. The needs of children there are still serious, but it's time to let the nationals run the next lap. There's nothing wrong with that."

Amanda, Jayla's old activist partner and still a firebrand, jumped in with a different view.

"It would be crazy to stop now when we have assets, stability, connections. Let's don't just quit. Let's reinvent ourselves. There's so much more good we can do."

Another board member nodded and started wondering out loud about expanding their orphanage work to neighboring Zambia or Zimbabwe, with perhaps more nations to come.

Still another suggested staying focused on Mozambique but shifting emphasis to primary education or children's health care.

"What do *you* think, Jayla?" asked Rev. Jeffers.

Jayla had been dreading that question, though she knew it would come. What was the best thing for CRM to do? Was it time to sunset itself? Or should it get ready for a rebirth of some kind?

And beyond that, she knew, the decision that the board would make would also determine her own future. She still had a good ten, maybe fifteen years of working life in her. Would she prefer to spend them in her adopted homeland or back in the States?

Right now, she told herself, *I've got to lead this board in making the decision to either start a new game or put the pieces back in the box. And I have no idea how to do it.*

- Tom and the pressure to take his company national
- Lane reacting to the disruption of digital publishing
- Dev and the option to try a completely different line of business
- Jayla trying to figure out if her NGO should even continue

These four men and women are like bosses, execs, and chiefs everywhere. They understand deep within their leader souls that they bear the responsibility for initiating strategy within their organizations. It's on them, and they take it seriously.

But at the same time these leaders are wrestling with changes in the spaces within which their organizations operate. They are, in some ways, unsure of how to lead their companies. The possibilities all seem so murky. Where should they be headed, and how do they get there? Is it even possible to know?

CHAPTER 2

HERE COMES
STRATEGY 3.0

I HAVE SEVERAL friends who have taken me sailboating over the years, and I've noticed something about how these skippers operate. When they're ready to head home, they will pick a landmark on the shore to direct their craft toward. But they don't head there at full speed in a straight line. They can't. The wind isn't blowing directly toward their destination. Other craft are crossing before their bows. So their course becomes a zigzag as they tack this way and that. They speed up and slow down as the wind and the waves shift. But despite all this, I've observed, my sailing friends manage to steadily make their way to the home dock.

It's much the same with strategy for businesses and nonprofits. The future is going to throw a lot of variety at us, demanding that we come up with inventive solutions. Our course won't be linear. But we can still have a goal in our line of sight and make our way toward it with agility and focus.

So if you're facing your own strategy dilemma, trust that it is possible to practice strategy successfully today. I'm going to show you how.

THE EVOLUTION OF STRATEGY

I see three major stages in the history of strategy.

Historians cite the Chinese military classic *The Art of War*, written by Sun Tzu around 500 B.C., as the first known work on strategy. And in fact, for a long time it was believed that war was the primary application for strategy. (Our word strategy comes from the Greek term *strategia*, meaning "generalship.") The goal was to conquer your enemy through deployment of resources in such a way that you won your prize intact and at acceptable cost to your own side.

After World War II, military planning migrated off the battlefield and into the offices of business and government as strategic planning. Experts such as Peter Drucker and Michael Porter developed theories to guide leaders in helping their organizations succeed.

These theories, produced at a time when the rate of social change was slower than it is now, provided a methodical way of thinking about setting goals and mobilizing employees to go after them. And it worked. Until it stopped working.

Strategy 3.0—starting now

Around the end of the twentieth century or the beginning of the twenty-first, conditions in society changed to the point that Strategy 2.0 began to falter in its effectiveness. Another strategic framework began to form in its place—one that isn't slow but fast, one that isn't systematic but agile. It's still possible to make smart decisions for our organizations that will pay off later. But now it calls for nimbleness, a tolerance for uncertainty, and the willingness to keep on trying until we get it right.

Leaders are desperate for a new kind of strategy that will work. The good news is that this strategic framework is already here. Strategy 3.0 will guide our thinking as we seek to make inspired choices for the good of our organizations and our customers.

TODAY'S STRATEGY REALITIES

If you're straining against the limitations of Strategy 2.0, then you need to understand how Strategy 3.0 differs from it. The new strategy reflects a separate set of realities out there in the world and inside our own organizations. Here are eight major contrasts between the two strategy paradigms at a glance:

STRATEGY 2.0	STRATEGY 3.0
Choices were limited.	*Choices are countless.*
Competition was evident.	*Competition is veiled.*
Information was safeguarded.	*Information is free and accessible.*
Predictability was reliable.	*Predictability is uncertain.*
The users of strategy were big companies.	*The users of strategy are everybody.*
The approach to strategy was systematic reverse-engineering.	*The approach to strategy is agile pivoting.*
The speed of strategy was slow.	*The speed of strategy is fast.*
The style of strategy was methodical.	*The style of strategy is adaptive.*

Let's look at each of these strategy realities more closely.

STRATEGY REALITY #1: CHOICES

Strategy 2.0: Choices were limited.
Strategy 3.0: Choices are countless.

Years ago, when you were ordering a cup of coffee, your choices were basically regular or decaf. Now your nearby Starbucks offers caffè misto, cinnamon dolce latte, espresso con panna, and many more hot and cold coffee drinks, adjusted skinnywise or otherwise according to your preference. And in fact, you might not even want to go to a national chain like Starbucks. With all the local coffee joints opening up, you might prefer to take your bean-water business to one of the many shops with roots in your own backyard. Each has its own multiplicity of offerings.

Not a coffee drinker? Then let's take toothpaste.

Either Crest or Colgate—just one variety of each—used to wind up on almost every toothbrush in America.

Now there are more than ninety varieties of toothpaste for sale, including whitening toothpastes, tartar-killing toothpastes, gingivitis-preventing toothpastes, herbal toothpastes, and toothpastes offering the assurance that no animals were harmed in their manufacture.

The number of products of all types on supermarket shelves has gone up 500 percent since the 1970s.[1]

Even the number of nonprofit organizations—offering their own "services and products" to attract your charitable dollars—has increased by 25 percent just since 2001.

In short, today the customer has grown accustomed to having a wide array of choices, often including free stuff.[2] Your strategic plans have to take into account all the alternatives you *could* offer and make the right decisions about what you *will* offer.

STRATEGY REALITY #2: COMPETITION

Strategy 2.0: Competition was evident.
Strategy 3.0: Competition is veiled.

It used to be obvious who the competition was. Pepsi was trying to take the fizz out of Coca-Cola. Hewlett-Packard wanted to push delete on Big Blue. Nike was just doing it to Reebok.

But today, competition can appear out of nowhere and take on surprising forms. Blockbuster wasn't ready for the advent of Netflix and Redbox. When the iPad appeared, people selling products as diverse as computers, e-readers, and game consoles all found they had an unexpected source of competition. Who would have thought the big-box retailers would be looking over their shoulder at the B2C online shopping monster Amazon as their biggest threat?

The drivers of unforeseen competition can include the emergence of new technology, mergers or alliances among companies, innovations in ordering systems or distribution channels, the discovery of new ways to cut costs and prices, and changes in consumer demographics.

A competitor could be a hyper-ambitious overreacher totally outside your space (in your mind), or it could be someone in your vertical who has painted the bull's-eye on your back.

Your strategy has to be flexible enough to permit your organization to react effectively at the first appearance of new competition. Or perhaps to make *you* the competition someone else never saw coming.

STRATEGY REALITY #3: INFORMATION

Strategy 2.0: Information was safeguarded.
Strategy 3.0: Information is free and accessible.

Once upon a time, companies jealously guarded information about their best practices, market penetration, software coding, and much more. *What we know that nobody else knows is what gives us the edge…*or so the thinking went.

But proprietary information is no longer the competitive advantage it used to be. That's because there is hardly any proprietary information anymore.

In the mid 1980s Stewart Brand famously declared, "Information wants to be free," and since then, that particular bit of prophecy has largely been fulfilled.

"NOWADAYS, YOU HAVE TO ACCOUNT FOR THE AVAILABILITY OF INFORMATION WHEN YOU'RE CHOOSING YOUR STRATEGY."

Knowledge of just about any matter is available online if you know the right keyword to type into a search engine. Although I have known for years now that we live in a search society, I am still astounded at how easy it is to find specific and useful information to fast-track my learning curve.

For example, do you want some ideas about setting up your distribution centers? Get a fast start by settling down with your laptop and reading up on the way that the giants such as Wal-Mart and Amazon have done it. Or keep searching until you find a company that's doing it well in your own backyard, and go to their plant to take a look for yourself.

Or do you want to know how to goose the creativity inside your organization? Google Google to find out how it's done in Cupertino.

And if you think you can control the information that others find out about *you*, good luck with that. It's not just the government that struggles to keep its internal information internal. Your own customers are going to be posting reviews about your products up and down the star range, whether you want them to or not.

Information is a bird that has flown the cage. Nowadays, you have to account for the availability of information when you're choosing your strategy.

STRATEGY REALITY #4: PREDICTABILITY

Strategy 2.0: Predictability was reliable.
Strategy 3.0: Predictability is uncertain.

Predictability is a quality that strategists have always prized. It gives them confidence in their ability to make plans that will position their organization to take advantage of the opportunities around the next corner and further down the road.

The problem is, predictability has slipped away. And it has taken strategic confidence away with it.

"The future is never defined, organized, boundaried, or anchored," writes Grant McCracken, getting poetical in a *Harvard Business Review* blog. "Really, it's all just hints and whispers. Fragile melody, no refrain."[3]

Some of the causes driving these changes include the appearance of new high-tech tools, shifts in social networks, increased globalization, and ever-quicker changes in consumer attitudes and preferences. These changes, if they don't exactly make predictions and forecasts obsolete, certainly make them less trustworthy than they used to be.

That's why Roger Martin, speaking at the Skoll World Forum, said, "Every model is wrong and every strategy is wrong. Strategy in a way helps you learn what is 'righter.' People think you can prove a strategy in advance. You can't."[4]

Today's strategists have to abandon their rigid focus on predictions, learn to rely more on insights than on analytical models, expect surprising outcomes, and stand ready to react swiftly to events as they unfold, prototyping and experimenting their way to success. Predictability is no longer probable.

STRATEGY REALITY #5: USERS

Strategy 2.0: The users of strategy were big companies.
Strategy 3.0: The users of strategy are everybody.

The 1950s, when Strategy 2.0 was born, was the great age of corporations and of what was then termed "the corporate man." The ones leading the way in strategy were execs at large corporations such as Boston Consulting Group (Bill Henderson), Bain & Co. (Bill Bain), and McKinsey & Co. (Fred Gluck).[5] It took an army of a company to implement the military-like strategies that were then being promulgated.

The picture today is radically changed.

It's not just big companies that are using strategy; small to medium-sized companies are discovering the importance of intentional reaching toward the future. And, in fact, these smaller companies may be the ones who are best suited for the agile, innovative style of strategy that works today.

Furthermore, it's not even just for-profit companies that employ strategy anymore. Nonprofit organizations, government agencies, political parties, sports teams, universities, churches, and other organizations are using strategy.

Even individuals are learning to use strategy for themselves. Sole proprietors, such as dentists and plumbers, are trying to get a line of sight on the future and some sense of where to direct resources and accept risk. People talk about their parenting strategies, investing strategies, and strategies of many other kinds.

The idea of strategy has permeated the globe.

If you have any doubts about whether you or your organization should bother with strategy, banish them now.

STRATEGY REALITY #6: APPROACH

Strategy 2.0: The approach to strategy was systematic reverse-engineering.
Strategy 3.0: The approach to strategy is agile pivoting.

In the 1950s and 1960s, five-year corporate planning documents were the hot new thing in strategy. Leaders would decide where they wanted their organization to be in five years, then systematically work backward to come up with plans for getting there. It was even rumored that in the old days, FedEx operated from a one-hundred-year strategic planning document!

As late as 1989, when Stephen Covey wrote *The Seven Habits of Highly Effective People*, he identified Habit 2 as "Begin with the end in mind." That's reverse-engineering in a nutshell.

And this approach made sense when social and business conditions were more stable than they are today. But systematic reverse-engineering doesn't work so well when conditions five years from now are barely imaginable, with unforeseen technologies, interests, and consumption patterns sure to pop up.

Having a reverse-engineered plan now feels like being chained to a strategy that could quickly become outdated. What's needed instead of long-range planning is an ability to pivot when conditions change and new opportunities suddenly appear.

In a recent IBM survey of more than 1,500 CEOs, the respondents identified creativity as the most important leadership quality. "Creative leaders," summarized the survey report, "are comfortable with ambiguity and experiment to create new business models. They invite disruptive innovation, encourage others to drop outdated approaches and take balanced risks."[6]

A big part of being creative is fostering a culture of entrepreneurship that's ready to try new things and take risks. Over and over again.

Groupon is an example of a company that learned to pivot. The company was birthed on an online activism platform. When that iteration went nowhere, the founders started a blog and experimented with their insight that coupon redemption could lead to group action. Starting with a promotion for a pizzeria in their own building, they quickly grew into a billion-dollar business. No five-year reverse-engineering plan would ever have envisioned that.

Leaders have to make sure that those in their organization are thinking about strategy differently. When conditions change or you have a new insight about how to do your work better, you have to be ready to turn on a dime.

STRATEGY REALITY #7: SPEED

Strategy 2.0: The speed of strategy was slow.
Strategy 3.0: The speed of strategy is fast.

In 1989, pioneering computer scientist Alan Kay declared that it takes at least ten years for an innovation to get from the lab or the drawing board into everyday life. That may have been true at the time, but no longer. To take just one example, Instagram was launched in October 2010 and registered its 100 millionth user just eighteen months later.

One article on business strategy said this: "The world has become a more turbulent place, where anyone with a new idea can put it into action before you can say 'startup' and launch widespread movements with a single Tweet."[7]

Slow loses.

Fast wins. Or at least it has a chance to.

Nearly every successful company today is a "fast company," as the magazine of that name puts it.

The telecom company Vodafone, with hundreds of millions of customers in India and other countries, has made speed a hallmark of its strategy. "In this industry, an organization that is sluggish will not be successful," says chief executive Vittorio Colao. "There is quite fearsome competition, and you have to be very flexible and nimble."[8]

It isn't just a matter of speeding up production or distribution processes, although that may help. Strategy itself has to speed up. We have to go from development of ideas, to the execution of them, to the evaluation of the results in a shorter period of time than ever before.

If Aesop lived today, he'd be telling the fable of the tortoise and the hare with a different ending.

STRATEGY REALITY #8: STYLE

Strategy 2.0: The style of strategy was methodical.
Strategy 3.0: The style of strategy is adaptive.

The mantra of strategy used to be "plan the work and work the plan." It was all about progress by stepwise motion. Consistency would win the day.

But what happens when change taking place in our competition space intervenes to render the plan irrelevant? To continue the method then would be madness.

You can't plod anymore. Nowadays, you have to learn to dance.

Cisco became the world leader in selling routers and networking equipment with a traditional hierarchical structure and methodical business practices. After the dotcom bust of the 1990s, however, it had to reinvent itself. It did this by creating cross-functional teams to help the company move with greater agility into diverse markets around the world.

Ikea is basically a home goods retailer. But when leaders in the company noticed that real estate values would shoot up in the vicinity of each store they opened in Russia, they came up with a plan to develop shopping malls around their stores. The company now makes more profit in Russia from these malls than it does by selling Swedish design for the masses. That's adapting to seize an opportunity.[9]

One reason Facebook overcame MySpace so quickly for leadership in social media was its early decision to open its social network platform to outside developers. At first tens of thousands, and then hundreds of thousands, of apps appeared on Facebook. "By creating a flexible and popular platform," commented Martin Reeves, "the company actively shaped the business environment to its own advantage rather than merely staking out a position in an existing market or reacting to changes, however quickly, after they'd occurred."[10] In other words, it was adaptive.

If you want to have effective strategies these days, you need to be really good at learning how to do new things and how to do old things in new ways. It takes being alert to signals of change from your environment. It takes a willingness to keep your planning cycles short and to experiment over and over again. And it takes a tolerance for failure, combined with a determination to keep on trying until you get it right.

Today, an effective strategy is one that is light on its feet.

THE NEW TOOLS OF STRATEGY

Long ago, people would scratch their words on rocks. Then there was soft clay and a stylus. Then paper and ink. Then a typewriter. Then a desktop or laptop or tablet computer.

The point? New days call for new tools.

Speed and agility are the new tools of strategy. Pick them up.

Of course, using Strategy 3.0 won't *guarantee* your success. You can move fast in the wrong direction. You can be agile and still not end up in the right spot.

But properly used, the tools of Strategy 3.0 give you your best chance to position your organization for success in the future. They enable you to tack your sailboat to the shore.

Right now, though, you probably have a lot of questions about how to actually operate as a 3.0 strategist. It's one thing to know the new realities of strategy; it's another to harness them to make decisions for your business or nonprofit.

The ultimate tool for strategy is the process that's coming up next.

CHAPTER 3

LEADING
STRATEGY

KODAK ONCE DOMINATED the photographic film industry—by the 1970s, capturing *90 percent* of the market! Yet in the 1990s, the company began to falter badly. Despite having invented the core technology used in digital cameras, Kodak failed to adequately make the transition from film photography to digital. Other companies created the products that people were using to take pictures of graduations and new babies, birthdays and Grandma.

In 2012, Kodak filed for Chapter 11 bankruptcy protection and set about selling off assets to try to get back in the black. As of this writing, the company seems to be hovering between stages four and five— "grasping for salvation" and "capitulating to irrelevance or death"—of Jim Collins' five stages of company decline.[1] The phrase "Kodak moment" will take on a whole new meaning if the company vanishes into history.

What happened here?

Kodak had a failure of strategy. When digital technology revolutionized photography, Kodak wasn't fast and focused. It wasn't agile and adaptive.

And this story is instructive for us. No matter how successful we may have been in the past, we can't get complacent about the future.

We always have to be working on strategies for the next stage and the one after that. We have to be like competitive mountain bikers, who say they "see through the curve."

But that raises a question—How?

How do you take a strategy from start to finish in a world filled with change and uncertainty?

EIGHT STEPS

There is a process that leaders today can use to lead their companies toward successful strategy. Its parts are recognizable from earlier eras, but it has twists and bends and reinterpretations that come from the nature of the new business realities. You might be surprised by its starting point. You might take a while to get used to its demands upon your imagination as well as upon your hardheaded business sense. You might feel your adrenaline surging when you see the way it requires you to make quick, bold decisions to turn the ship of strategy, or issue an all-engines-stop order, or call for full speed ahead.

But literally, there's no other way to come up with strategy effectively in today's world (unless you get really lucky).

This is how you create 3.0 strategy for your organization.

There are eight parts to this process (though nobody will use all eight parts for any one strategy). Together, they create an entire taxonomy or ecosystem of strategy.

+ The first four parts of the process take you from gathering information to settling on and testing out a new strategy. You will need to follow all four of these steps in sequence.
+ The final four parts of the process comprise a set of options you can choose from, depending upon the feedback you get to your early strategy. You'll choose just one of these options.

Working this process will give you the clarity you want about what's next for your organization or business unit.

Let's take a look at the process in more detail, piece by piece. As you're reading about this process, let it stir up ideas in your mind for how you can put it into practice within your organization for the particular strategic needs you have today.

CONVERSATION

▼

INSIGHTS

▼

CHOICES

▼

FEEDBACK

❙❙	↻	✕	↗
PAUSE	PIVOT	PULL THE PLUG	POWER UP

CONVERSATION

The old days of an executive cooking up the future for his organization by sitting alone in an office and cruising through spreadsheets are gone.

Strategy creation in a 3.0 world looks very different. It's not solitary but collaborative. It's not based solely on hard data. It's derived in large part from human conversation.

In a world where change is endemic and uncertainty may be the only certainty, what you want is an insight solid enough to build a product, a service, a brand, a marketing campaign, or a whole company around. Somebody within your reach has that insight. You get to it by talking until it comes out.

Here's why: we live in a storytelling culture. Our stories are not just fiction but also are factual narratives. And storytelling is not just for entertainment but seeps into all areas of life. In recent years, experts such as Peter Guber, author of *Tell to Win*, have demonstrated the value of storytelling in business.[2]

Storytelling is not just a gimmick or an add-on.

Steve Denning writes in *Forbes* magazine, "The ongoing reinvention of management to transform workplaces from the boring, sterile, dispiriting cubicles of the 20th Century into the lively centers of inspiration and creativity that are needed for the Creative Economy of the 21st Century has storytelling at its core."[3]

Conversation is the proper starting point of 3.0 strategy because it allows people to tell their stories. Valuable insights come out of these stories that would be most unlikely to come out of mere data.

As told to me by an executive of an agency connected with the project, Procter & Gamble found a compelling and unexpected insight about how to reach burqa-wearing women in Saudi Arabia for their cosmetic product Oil of Olay. At first P&G had approached marketing Oil of Olay in this Middle Eastern country by touting the traditional skin benefits of anti-aging. Sales flagged. What was needed was a conversation with these women to find out more about their lives.

The agency went exploring to find the insights. By befriending a few families and simply becoming part of their daily lives, they eventually were invited into conversation about cosmetics.

During the conversation, these Saudi women lowered their burqas to reveal the beautifully painted faces that they proudly protected to share with their husbands. They confided that they "loved" Oil of Olay because it helped them create a "clean canvas."

The epiphany about how the product was used completely changed the positioning of Oil of Olay in the Saudi market. Data and research reports alone would never have revealed this insight to P&G. The insight was revealed through conversation and led to a turnaround in sales for the brand.

Conversation is like a field where you are tilling the soil to get something to grow.

For example, recently I was advising a global nonprofit on its process for growing into the future. My suggestion to them was to hold some discussions on the topics they wanted clarity on with four key groups—leadership, lower-level staff, people they serve, and outside advisers. These aren't bull sessions. The discussion is kept within guardrails; it's *about* something.

That's how one organization is doing it. Another company or nonprofit might choose to conduct its conversations differently.

They can be formal or informal, highly structured or somewhat looser, carried out in-house or out of house, involving just the team or bringing in outsiders.

The important thing is that it's the right people talking about the right topic. It's a guided dialogue designed to allow opinions to come out so that the strategy leaders can begin to understand what's happening in their world and what their organization might do next. Instead of mining data, you're mining conversation. And in the process you're giving the participants a sense of having a say and of knowing what's going on.

Stage enough conversations to till enough of the soil until valuable opinions and comments begin to grow.

Tips to have an effective conversation:
- Practice active listening skills. This means using more open-ended questions, repeating, paraphrasing, and reflecting with follow-up.
- Use the words *why* and *how* more often than you use *who, what, when,* and *where.*
- Put meaningful dialogue into time lines and sequence.
- Be sure to get context and back story.

INSIGHT

Holding conversations on the right topics with the right people tills the ground so that a lot of perspectives quickly grow. The next step is to glean at least one ripe insight from the harvest that has the potential to carry a new strategy.

And just as it's amazing how one kernel or seed can grow an entire plant, It's incredible how one insight can carry a product or a company for an entire season.

Insight: Everybody brushes their teeth, and many would like a spinning brush similar to the one the dentist uses on them. But back in the 1990s, the spinning brushes on the market cost at least $70— more than most people were willing to spend.

Response: Inventor John Osher put together the battery-operated SpinBrush using technology he had already created, selling each brush for a mere $5. (He soon sold the business for $475 million.)

Insight: Zeneca Ag Products had a promotion program that it thought was a value proposition for its customers. But its customers started saying they didn't like the way the complicated program was eating up their time.

Response: Zeneca dropped the promotion and made more money.

Insight: Just about every home has a hard floor that has to be cleaned. But conversations with homeowners revealed frustration because mops are messy and difficult.

Response: P&G developed Swiffer in 1999. It's still one of their most profitable products, with numerous spin-offs.

Would you love to have a transformative insight like these come out of your conversations? Just one could make your business.

When it happens, it may come as a sudden *Aha!* moment. More likely, though, it will come out of a methodical process of listening, talking, and learning.[4] That's why I encourage planned conversations. *Make an epiphany happen. Don't just wait for it.*

Do you see how different this kind of insight seeking is from data mining? What you're after is a *human* truth about the way people act or what they desire. This takes an ability to see inside the human heart and mind.

"WHEN IT HAPPENS, IT MAY
COME AS A SUDDEN *AHA!*
MOMENT. MORE LIKELY,
THOUGH, IT WILL COME OUT OF
A METHODICAL PROCESS
OF LISTENING, TALKING,
AND LEARNING."

I have often jokingly said, "I'll trade you three data analysts for one anthropologist." But as a matter of fact, hiring someone trained in business anthropology (a real branch of this academic discipline) is becoming common. That's because these people know how to read the behavioral tendencies of consumers.

Chip maker Intel hired Genevieve Bell, an anthropologist with a Ph.D., to help the company make choices about new products. She spends most of her time in homes and other places where people gather all over the world, talking to them about how they use technology. For example, according to one magazine profile, she "fought hard to get chip designers to rethink their impulse to build ever-faster processors and market them outside the U.S. For great swaths of the world the Internet is, and will continue to be, mostly text on a phone, she says. And so Intel is pursuing that market with its Atom chips, which are cheaper and consume less power than, say, Intel Core i3 or Celeron processors."[5]

Of course, it's not only anthropologists or other trained social science professionals who can find insights. Anybody with a trace of empathy can find insights. You can find insights.

Here is where your expertise as a leader comes into play. You don't dream up strategy alone in your office, but you do apply your experience and judgment in evaluating the insights that you gather through conversations.

Treasure them when you get them. They're not only as growth producing as kernels—they're as valuable as nuggets of gold.

Tips to bubble up insights in conversation:
- Listen for emotion—phrases that indicate desire, dream, defeat, or discouragement.
- Look for patterns, trends, and consequential facts.
- Discern what comes naturally to someone, and where the natural momentum of the organization is, and probe around the corner from that.
- Do an OT analysis—like SWOT but focused solely on opportunities and threats (that's where insights often come from).[6]

CHOICE

Jim Collins and Morten T. Hansen begin their book *Great by Choice* by stating, "We cannot predict the future. But we can create it."[7]

How do we create the future? By making choices that will get us where we want to go.

I can't tell you how many times I've seen strategy processes that didn't wind up going anywhere. The energy all went sideways. Maybe even backwards. That's because the people involved didn't have the guts or the discipline to make a choice and go with it.

The whole purpose of holding the conversations and gathering insights is so that you can pass through the gates of decision. So as soon as you have found an idea that you believe holds potential for success, you have to make a choice about the specific strategy you will pursue to realize that potential.

The kind of choice we're talking about is not merely a decision. It's also the action that follows. We might refer to it as a "choiceful action."

You're a real estate broker and you had the *insight* that people want to see inside the houses that are on the market before they take the time to visit in person.

You *decide* that it's worth seeing if you could get more business by putting video of home interiors on your website. You *act* by sending out a videographer to take 360-degree video of rooms in a few of your listings to see what reaction you get.

You're a natural gas distributor and you had the *insight* that interest in natural gas as a fuel for vehicles is finally becoming serious. You *decide* that the way to get into this market is to form a partnership with a filling station chain. You *act* by negotiating a deal with one of these chains and delivering compressed natural gas in a limited market to gauge the reaction.

So "Choice" is the step where the strategy process becomes more concrete. You create a document outlining your strategy. You marshal your resources, develop tactics, and execute a plan to put your strategy into operation.

Whatever you do, it requires a choice. And making a choice always requires courage. So you may be nervous about committing resources to a strategy that may fail. Remember that in a fast-moving economy there are hidden costs to doing nothing and remaining stagnant. Remember, too, that good decision making is a skill you can develop through learning and practice.[8]

Without decision, you can find yourself marching in place or just milling about. Take a step of progress. It may be a baby step, but at least it will be forward motion.

Tips to make a good strategic choice:

+ Limit yourself to three people to run your idea by—fewer and you have a blind spot, more and you'll be paralyzed by options.
+ Play out your theory of change—who and what will be impacted by your decision.
+ Do a cost/benefit analysis, but do it for three years down the road.
+ Sleep on it. If possible, practice the twenty-four-hour rule of waiting before taking the decisive step.
+ Push the button on the choice. Make the decision.

FEEDBACK

You may have already discerned this phenomenon:
Because you're the boss, when you ask people whether
they like something you've come up with, they say,
"Yes, yes, yes" like an eager puppy. Is that their real
opinion? It's hard to know. (And if you're vain or
lacking in self-assurance, you may secretly crave the
validation whether or not it's reliable.)

But look, when you've launched a new strategy,
the last thing you want is this kind of sucking-up
response. You need objective, reliable data, whether
it strokes your ego or not. You've got to let the world
push on your strategy so that you can see if it holds up
against the pressure.

Feedback can come from many sources. Social
media. Surveys. Sales figures. Pay-per-click
advertising. Focus groups. Sales associate debriefings.
More conversations.

A daily deals website called 1SaleADay.com started
selling a utility knife that folds into the size of a credit
card. The company leaders were taken aback when one
person posted on their website, "As a law enforcement
officer, I do not appreciate you selling items that
criminals can easily hide."[9]

Instead of immediately reacting to this negative unsolicited feedback, the company decided to get *more* feedback. In a Facebook post, they asked their large body of followers what they thought about the company selling the credit card knife. Within twenty-four hours, they had received 750 comments. The majority agreed with the decision to sell the knife. Result? A decision was reinforced. (Not to mention, a potential crisis was turned into positive PR.)

Just as you needed to conduct the original strategic conversations with the right people on the right topics, so now you need to get feedback from the right people on the right questions about your strategy.

Here is where the data analysts come into their own. There are usually numbers to crunch, spreadsheets to create, graphs to put on SlideRocket. Yet you also need "soft" analysis. You still need not just numbers but also the ability to discern human factors such as trends, patterns, and excitement levels.

One caution: Be on the lookout for false positives. It's not just employees looking to butter up the boss who sometimes say what you want to hear. Research has shown repeatedly that respondents to surveys and similar feedback instruments tend to inflate their opinion of a product or service.

Just because nine out of ten survey respondents say they like your new app doesn't mean that will translate into nine out of ten paying money for it. Just because all your friends love your idea for a community third space doesn't mean you will be able to raise the money.

Don't rely on yes-men. Get some professional assistance, if needed, to make sure the feedback you're getting is as reliable as it can be.

Tips to get feedback you can use:
- Give employees freedom to be generous in correcting consumer complaints; this action encourages more feedback over the years to come.
- Research your company on Google, Facebook, and other relevant sites, and see what people are saying about you. Then try to keep the conversation moving.
- Develop an insider group of people who *like* you *and* will tell you the truth; offer them perks for their involvement.
- Make sure someone has the responsibility for compiling customer feedback into a readable format in order to present it as fodder for insight.

Once you have a solid basis of feedback, and you believe it's reliable, then you need to do what may be the hardest thing of all: act accordingly. I summarize the four responses you can take with four P's. You need to decide to *pause, pivot, pull the plug,* or *power up.* This isn't a sequence. You choose any one of these at a time.

PAUSE

Even though the feedback you got on your choice is encouraging, you still might decide to wait before implementing your new strategy. This isn't procrastination we're talking about here. This is pausing—pulling over to the side of the road for a while before moving on.

I talked with a client recently who has a promising plan for expansion but has decided to hold off on it until his cash catches up with him. In a little while his company will be in a solid financial position to move ahead with the growth strategy, and so it makes sense for him to wait until then.

That's just one reason for pausing. There are many others. You might need to gather your human resources before advancing your strategy further. You might need to wait for conditions in your industry to become more auspicious. You might want to let a competitor blow through its marketing budget to create the market momentum you need to build on top of. Or you might need to get your personal footing with priorities in place.

Don't be afraid to put your strategy on Pause if that seems smart to you. When you're ready to hit the Play button, it will be all the more successful.

Tips when taking a strategic pause:
+ Make sure you are still leading through the pause phase. Pausing is not the same as going to sleep.
+ Identify the time frame or the conditions that will pull you back into the game.
+ Remember, timing is often more important than time.
+ Take stock. Look back on the road you have traveled. Pauses are a great time for reflection.

What if your feedback tells you that your choiceful action is only a qualified success? You have to take that feedback seriously and do something about it. One obvious option is that you change your planned course and try something else. In a word, you pivot.[10]

Pivoting is the essence of agility. Let's see what it looks like.

In 2011 J.C. Penney, a once-iconic department store chain that had been fading in popularity, hired Apple retail expert Ron Johnson as CEO and proceeded to give its stores a new look. Choice. Very quickly, customer complaints began pouring in and sales headed over a cliff. *Feedback—definite feedback!* So the board fired Johnson, rehired its previous CEO, and revisited the changes they had made to their stores. Pivot.

A J.C. Penney television commercial directly addressing the failed strategy showed that the leaders knew the value of trying again after failure. "Some changes you liked," it said, "and some you didn't. But what matters with mistakes is what we learn. Come back to J.C. Penney. We heard you."[11]

It remains to be seen whether Penney's pivot will work or whether this department store will go the way of Montgomery Ward and Woolworth's. But the company deserves credit for moving fast when its strategy proved a failure.

All kinds of other companies—large, small, and medium sized, offering services or making products—have had to pivot in their own ways.

One magazine article summed up some of the most notable pivots executed in recent years:

Before Twitter became a microblogging sensation it was a podcasting business. YouTube's founders were convinced they'd hit the jackpot with a video-dating site. PayPal's original mission was to beam IOUs from Palm Pilot to Palm Pilot. Flickr grew out of a massive multiplayer online game as a way for players to drop photos into text messages. Instagram's founders created a check-in technology called Blurbn before settling on photos. Pandora was a B2B music recommendation service. Yelp transitioned from email recommendations from friends to a local search and user review website.[12]

If your organization needs to pivot like these companies, here's how you do it: You return to an earlier step in the strategy process.

Maybe your strategic insight was a good one but the choice you made to act on that insight wasn't effective. Go back to the choice box and try a different approach. Instead of left, go right.

Or if you think there's a more fundamental problem with your strategy, go back even further in the process. You might want to review the data that came out of your conversations and see if you can come up with a better insight to act upon. You might even want to start all over with new conversations.

Go back in the process as far as you have to go in order to step onto a different course that will lead to a better destination.

Here's another way of looking at it. There is a time for *disruptive innovation*—creating an all-new playing field. And there is a time for *iterative innovation*—making a new play call to try to move the ball down the field better. Pivoting is a way to produce iterative innovation.

If there's still hope for your overall strategy, don't give up. Learn from your mistakes and keep on trying. A willingness to make a quick turn and perform on-the-spot innovation—to pivot—can help you locate the place in today's unpredictable market where rewards are waiting for you.

Tips for pivoting in your strategy:
+ Make sure to create an agile culture within your organization. (This is no easy assignment.)
+ Think precisely. There will be some things you want to retain while you'll want to pivot on.
+ Revisit each of the four original steps (conversation, insight, choice, and feedback) and complete this sentence: "If I had to do it over again, I would _____." Pay special attention to insight and choice.

What piece of the business (no matter how small) is the one that has the most momentum and/or makes the most money?

PULL THE PLUG

If the feedback you get on your intended strategy is strongly negative, there's no point in pausing or pivoting to try to make it work. It's better to pull the plug and move on to something completely different.

This is an obvious choice, yet I've found that pulling the plug is a hard call for a lot of people to make when it comes to their own business strategies.

Large corporations can pull the plug on a particular strategy easily enough, because they've got a lot else going on. But for small- and medium-sized companies, and especially for entrepreneurs, it's harder, because they've got so much of their resources tied up in a single strategy. Even if a strategy's prospects are looking dismal, its originators are tempted to try to make it work somehow rather than to disband the attack formation and regroup somewhere else on the battlefield.

I encourage the entrepreneurs I work with to learn the discipline of saying, "Enough!" about their unsuccessful strategies. It might feel like they're strangling their own baby, but often it's the right thing to do. I cite to them what is known in Hollywood as the "Adrien Brody Rule."

Adrien Brody is the reedy actor best known for his role in *The Pianist*. In 1998 the acclaimed director Terrence Malick cast Brody in his World War II film *The Thin Red Line*. It's Malick's courage in making this film that established the Adrien Brody Rule.

After paying Brody's substantial salary and shooting the entire movie, Malick decided to reconceive the story in the editing room. The director reviewed the footage, restructured the plot, and changed the narrative perspective. He ditched Brody the movie star for Brody the cameo actor by cutting most of Brody's scenes. In pursuit of the best film he could make, Malick fearlessly scrapped months of work and bruised Brody's ego.

Robert Safian, the editor of *Fast Company* magazine, explains the lesson of Malick's bold move this way: "You can't make decisions based on initial assumptions or the amount of resources extended, but solely on what best meets the needs of the situation."[13] That's the Adrien Brody Rule.

Now, I realize that on any project a thin red line separates the decision to stay the course and the decision to abandon the chase. Sometimes courageous commitment to keep going can finally yield results.

Yet equally, foolhardy stubbornness can lead to bankruptcy. After you've completed the analysis of your early strategy and zeroed in on an answer to how effective it was, don't be afraid to walk away from a losing gamble even if you've already invested considerable time, effort, and resources.[14]

I, personally, have made a commitment in recent years to pull the plug on ventures that aren't working. Just this year, I have killed off three businesses that I co-started. Each of them had been in operation about two years, and none of them had performed up to expectations, so I euthanized them. I've got more successful projects that I could be spending my time and resources on. So goodbye to these three businesses.

Contrary to what your high school coach might have told you, quitters sometimes win.

Tips on pulling the plug:

+ Write down the two or three nonnegotiables that mean you should shut down. These should be hard numbers (for example, "I will hit the kill switch if sales don't reach $_____," or "...if I don't raise $_____").

- Analyze your cash flow for the past year and project out for the next year.
- Ask yourself, What are the *three pivots I could make?* If none of these excite you with the possibilities they present, then pull the plug.
- Identify the costs (financial, relational, emotional) of pulling the plug. How will you weather those?

"DON'T BE AFRAID TO WALK AWAY FROM A LOSING GAMBLE EVEN IF YOU'VE ALREADY INVESTED CONSIDERABLE TIME, EFFORT, AND RESOURCES."

This is the simplest action option of all…and the most exciting. If the feedback you received for your choice is overwhelmingly positive, and if you're in a position to make it happen, then you need to do the opposite of pulling the plug on your strategy. You need to power it up.

Bet the farm on your winner of a strategy.

Karl Stark and Bill Stewart, co-founders of the strategic advisory firm Avondale, wrote about doubling down on investments. They said,

> Placing bets is part of any entrepreneurial, growth-oriented mindset. All the entrepreneurial superstars over time, from Henry Ford to Bill Gates to Larry Page and Sergey Brin, created rapid growth for their companies by making strategic bets and investing heavily. These pioneers didn't just make one good bet—they hit the jackpot year after year. In other words, they doubled down to create growth by reinvesting the profits of the company into cementing their competitive position and developing new growth avenues.[15]

If you believe in your strategy, throw your resources behind it and plan to make it pay off big. Expect great things and go after them.

But remember, this is a fast world. No matter how successful your strategy is, you'll need another one before long. Soon it will be time for more conversations, so that you can start the strategy process all over again.

Tips on powering up a strategy that can pay off big:

+ Make sure to count all of the costs in the expansion.
+ Commit to using your profits (and not just outside money) to invest in the business.
+ Clearly identify the two or three key mountains yet to be crossed.
+ Analyze the motivation and skill sets of your team. Do you need to gas up before you push down on the pedal?

PARTICULARIZING THE PROCESS

First, stage some *conversations* and harvest the potential-filled insights that come out of them. Then make a choice about an action that could capitalize on an insight, and put it into operation. Once you get some reliable *feedback* on how your new venture is going, choose to *pause* (delay temporarily before proceeding any further), *pivot* (make a strategy change within your overall vision), *pull the plug* (quit on a losing strategy), or *power up* (go full bore with a winner).

That's the Strategy 3.0 process. It works. It will work for you. But remember that it's not a rigid equation. There's no one always-right way to implement it. Invest the framework with your own personality, adapt it to the culture of your organization, and target it for the strategic need lying before you. Use it in your own way to create forward momentum for your particular organization.

If you've still got qualms and reservations (*What if we ignored some key variables? What downstream effects are we overlooking?*), that's normal. There's no way of eliminating all the risk from strategy in a 3.0 world. But there is a way of *minimizing* the risk.

"FIRST, STAGE SOME
CONVERSATIONS AND HARVEST
THE POTENTIAL-FILLED
INSIGHTS THAT COME OUT OF
THEM. THEN MAKE A CHOICE
ABOUT AN ACTION THAT COULD
CAPITALIZE ON AN INSIGHT,
AND PUT IT INTO OPERATION."

CHAPTER 4

TEST-DRIVING
YOUR STRATEGY

GROUP INSURER UNUM tried to achieve growth by merging with Provident, an individuals insurer. But the costs and complications of trying to unite the two sales forces proved insuperable. Too bad Unum didn't insure the deal, because it cost them dearly. They experienced a 30 percent drop in stock price before they managed to undo the merger.[1] *Failed strategy.*

Motorola invested $5 billion in producing satellite telephones that came with a price tag of $3,000 each, not including the hefty monthly fee. In the process, the company ignored evidence about the shortcomings of their technology and about market resistance to the consumer cost. Customers hung up on the offering in droves. Within a year, this business line was in Chapter 11. *Failed strategy.*

School bus operator Laidlaw thought they would be building on their core competencies by getting into the ambulance business. But the company wasn't prepared for dealing with the technical and legal complexities of the medical industry. The ambulance operation quickly went code blue, and Laidlaw had to get out of it at a loss. *Failed strategy.*

If you don't want your strategy showcased in the Strategic Hall of Infamy, or even just to fall short of your hopes for it, then my advice is to try to anticipate what could go wrong before you take it too far. When you know the risks, you can take steps to mitigate them—or even scrap the strategy altogether if it proves unworkable.

This chapter will show you how to subject your strategy to a diagnostic procedure to see if it's in shape to go to work for you. I call it test-driving your strategy.

FOUR-WHEEL DRIVE

In the early days of Internet car sales, I was interested in a car listed online for sale in Dallas. It so happened that I was going to have a layover in Dallas–Fort Worth on my way to another destination. I arranged for the owner of the car to bring it to the airport, where I got in the vehicle and took it out on the road. It turned out that this was one sweet ride. Because of the test-drive, I was confident in saying I would buy the car and wanted it delivered to my home in Fayetteville.

That's what we need to do before we're fully committed to our strategies. Take them out for a spin.

Specifically, what I'm saying is this: think through how the strategy you have in mind is likely to affect your organization in four key areas:

1. your customers
2. your people
3. your offering
4. your financials

These four elements are universal for all organizations—large and small, old and new, for profit and not for profit. Furthermore, like the wheels on a four-wheel-drive car, they all need to be engaged and working properly if you want to get maximum traction in a slippery patch on your journey.

Of course you can't foresee exactly how your strategy will impact these four areas. But carry out as rigorous an analysis as you can, and it may turn up some problems you've got to address as you move ahead in implementation.

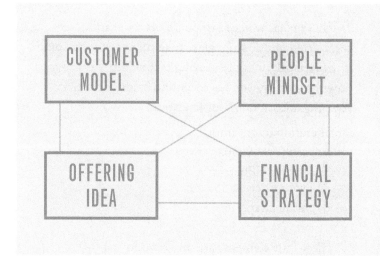

CUSTOMER MODEL

Every organization has customers, even if you don't refer to them as such in your organization. They may be clients, buyers, consumers, patients, patrons, members, investors, lenders, stakeholders, donors, or supporters. Regardless of what they're called, these are people who are external to your organization and who are making a decision about your value proposition. Their purchase or donation counterbalances your costs to do business.

Consequently, they are crucial to your operation. In your promotional material, you very well may claim that they are the reason for your operation.

All of which makes it absolutely necessary that you think through how the strategy you have under consideration might impact your customers.

Let's say your company made its name selling personal care products to women. Now, you're entertaining the possibility of branching out into men's products. Is there a danger that men will feel uncomfortable being associated with your brand? Might your long-time customers think you're no longer as committed to women?

Or imagine that you're leading a technology company.

You have a new vision to become the Henry Ford of home security, using your own technology to provide low-cost security options to low- and middle-income folks and not just the higher-wage earners with a case of nerves who usually install home security systems. What resistance are you going to encounter in taking an offering to a body of potential customers who aren't used to buying such a service?

Whatever kind of organization you have, and whatever strategy you're itching to put into place, you'd better try to anticipate beforehand how it's going to affect that group of people who make your organization's existence possible—your customers. Get some reliable customer feedback so that you can get a line on consumer thinking. Figure out what, if anything, you can do to make sure they're happy with the changes that are coming.

Ask yourself...
+ What will this strategy do to impact our legacy customers (those folks we have built the last few years on)?
+ How might this strategy help us or hurt us with the new customer segments we are chasing?
+ Where will the new strategy expose us to customer push-back?
+ Which customers will need special hand holding through the strategy implementation period?
+ How will this strategy make us think about our customers differently? In other words, how will our customer engagement model change?

PEOPLE MINDSET

A new strategy is rarely human resources neutral. It's going to offer advantages to, and put stresses on, the employees. What will be the impact of your strategy on your people? Or flip it: What will be the impact of your people on your strategy?

An unmotivated team is totally different from a motivated team. Consider how the changes you have in mind for your organization are likely to affect people top to bottom. They're not cogs. They won't automatically and uncomplainingly start turning in the opposite direction just because you ask them to.

Before you go ahead with any new strategy, ask yourself some questions like these:

If your literacy nonprofit is going to expand from giving away free books to starting a mentorship program in poor neighborhoods, how will your staffing needs change?

If you've decided to open a customer service node in India, how will the rest of your employees interact with these long-distance partners?

If you're planning to shift software engineers off their long-term project and onto something different, how will they react? What support will they need?

Taking the human factor into consideration is both kind and good for business. Avoid mismatches between strategy and management.

Ask yourself...

+ How will this strategy impact our most valuable leaders and managers?
+ Do we need different talent to pull off this strategy? Where specifically are our people gaps?
+ What new training and/or intelligence is necessary to successfully implement this strategy?
+ Is our current culture supportive of the strategy or running counterproductive to it?
+ Do we need to revamp our reward and comp system to ensure success?

"WHATEVER KIND OF ORGANIZATION YOU HAVE, AND WHATEVER STRATEGY YOU'RE ITCHING TO PUT INTO PLACE, YOU'D BETTER TRY TO ANTICIPATE BEFOREHAND HOW IT'S GOING TO AFFECT THAT GROUP OF PEOPLE WHO MAKE YOUR ORGANIZATION'S EXISTENCE POSSIBLE—YOUR CUSTOMERS."

OFFERING IDEA

Your offering is the *what* that you do, the product(s) or service(s) your people provide to your customers. It may include everything from price, to package, to brand, to functionality, to more. Yet it's usually easy to boil an organization's many activities down to a core offering.

H&R Block offers tax preparation.

McDonald's offers fast food.

Your local humane society offers animal protection.

Your dentist offers tooth care.

Any new strategy of consequence is going to affect your offering. But in what way? The greater your clarity on this, the less risk.

Famously, when Coca-Cola got rid of "old Coke" to replace it with "new Coke," they messed with an offering that millions of people liked as it was. The company's face was as red as its can when they brought back the older formula, rebranded as "Coca-Cola Classic." That's a pivot that wouldn't have been necessary if the company had been more careful with its offering in the first place.

There are slight changes to an offering and there are huge ones. There are positive changes and there are negative ones. Consider your offering a treasure you must preserve and polish. Make sure you're taking carefully calculated moves with the product or service you are known by.

Ask yourself...
+ In what ways does this new strategy reinforce our current core offering?
+ In what ways will our core offering be at risk with the new strategy?
+ What part of our offering will have to either be stopped or be reengineered to align with our strategy?
+ How will the strategy realign us vis-à-vis our competitors and their core offerings?

Finally, when it comes to test-driving your strategy, follow the money. Put the strategy through its economic paces with projections and analysis.

As you do so, be careful of the age-old blind spot of being too conservative with expenses (*It will not cost us that much*) and too liberal with revenues (*It's going to generate big numbers*). Behavioral economists point out that people in business tend to be too optimistic. One article on the subject stated, "Other than professional pessimists such as financial regulators, we all tend to be optimistic, and our forecasts tend toward the rosier end of the spectrum."[2]

The same article described how an investment bank in the early years of the twenty-first century tested its strategy against a pessimistic scenario—the market conditions of 1994, when a downturn lasted nine months. They accordingly built in some extra safety margin. But when the financial collapse of 2008–09 came along, they weren't ready for the severity of what they faced and had to make dramatic cuts to their cost base.

Crunch the numbers now lest they crunch you later.

Ask yourself…

+ Can our existing budget support the strategy?
+ How will we fund the new strategy?
+ How long will it take to get momentum and a return?
+ What are the current cash position and the forecasted cash position for the next season?

GREEN LIGHT

If your business or nonprofit is at a crossroads, your strategy will tell you which way to go. If you have taken that strategy out for a test-drive and have made adjustments so that all four wheels are working, then you've got a green light to start accelerating.

Strategy 3.0 will help you navigate the uncertainties of the world we live in. Be fast and focused. Be agile and adaptive.

The future is yours.

CHAPTER 5

A STRATEGY LEXICON

WHENEVER I TALK with leaders about the new way to do strategy, I find there are certain terms I can't avoid using. They keep coming out of my mouth because they're essential for describing the qualities and actions that make up the 3.0 strategist's experience.

Some of these keywords have already popped up in this book. Others may be new to you. I'm giving them to you here—along with description, examples, and business-tested advice—in alphabetical order, not in order of importance. The reality is, they're *all* important for you to know and to incorporate into your own language of leadership.

Agility: *When the environment is filled with movement, a leader has to be able to pounce and dodge.*

Many video games take you through a digital terrain where dangers pop up unexpectedly and rewards suddenly appear for the taking. Level by level, the stakes become riskier, the point totals get larger, and the action gets faster. One wrong move, and the fun can be over in an instant.

Maybe it's a good thing so many of today's younger leaders grew up playing video games, because the business landscape is getting more like a gamescape all the time. Threats hurtle toward us. Opportunities seem elusive but are there for you if you're quick enough to snatch them.

The point is, in this kind of world you've got to be agile.

For the purposes of Strategy 3.0, I would define agility as *the ability to act and react both rapidly and effectively according to the changes in your organization's environment.* Agility is the sister of adaptability, the first cousin of flexibility and nimbleness. It is as alert as a watchdog about what's coming near. It's as poised as a tightrope walker traversing a line while balancing imbalances. It's as versatile as a thoroughbred making its way through the straights and obstacles of a steeplechase course.

If you dither over your decisions, or have the reaction time of a three-toed sloth, you may be on your way to extinction. McGill University management guru Karl Moore describes the kinds of leaders needed now and in the future:

Today's organizational leaders are facing accelerating rates of volatility, uncertainty, complexity and ambiguity, all of which are showing no signs of slowing down. Whether it is the continuing digital revolution or expanding global markets, our current environment requires a constant state of innovation. For companies to continue succeeding, next generation leaders must be able to handle any curve ball thrown their way. Leading through this new business environment requires the capability to sense and respond to changes in the business environment with actions that are focused, fast and flexible. The best way to put it: next generation leaders have to be *agile*.[1]

In 2001, Emirates Airlines didn't have any immediate plans to add to its fleet. But then, when air travel in the United States and Europe took an unexpected dip following the 9/11 disaster, Emirates put in an order for the new A380 aircraft that Airbus was suddenly having trouble selling. The carrier got several new planes at bargain prices. That's agility.

When the advent of digital photography threatened Fujifilm's business model, the company launched a line of cosmetics products using technology it had developed for film.

Today, Astalift is one of the leading brands of anti-aging skin care and supplement products around the world. That's agility too.

So, how agile are you?

Believe it or not, it's possible to be *too* agile. Some leaders are trying to take their organizations through so many different changes so quickly that they're seen as Whiplash Bob or Betty by their nervous, exhausted teams. Effective leaders are flexible; they're not frenetic. Be ready to make a swift move, but be thoughtful and coordinated about it.

But then it's also possible to not be agile enough. Maybe you're change averse by nature. Maybe you've been doing business more or less the same way so long that it's hard to even imagine doing it differently. Either way, you can *develop* agility. Like a stiff-muscled athlete doing stretching exercises before an event, warm up by practicing agility in smaller-stakes strategies before trying it out where it matters more.

Perhaps you can bring your whole organization with you on a journey toward greater agility.

"EFFECTIVE LEADERS
ARE FLEXIBLE; THEY'RE
NOT FRENETIC. BE READY
TO MAKE A SWIFT MOVE,
BUT BE THOUGHTFUL AND
COORDINATED ABOUT IT."

Buy-in: *Over time, people only implement what they understand and what they believe in.*

Any parent knows you get a better response from children when you take time to explain why a desired behavior is important and win their cooperation than when you issue orders like a drill sergeant.

If this is true with children, how much more with grown-up employees?

The riskiest and most expensive implementation is the one that is mindless, with passionless people carrying out a strategy while being either heavily policed or bribed to stay on task. And that's why, between a strategy's creation and its execution, there lies a step you can't afford to skip—making allies of everyone else within your organization for the new strategy.

Before you can expect the others in your business or nonprofit to make your idea a reality, you've got to present it to them in such a way that they can grasp it and accept it. In fact, you want them fired up about it! You want them not just willing but eager to come on board the sailboat you'll be tacking to the destination.

You know the leaders own the strategy. After all, they created it. But the rest of the team have to own it too. That's buy-in.

In the mid 1990s, Hamot Health Foundation of Erie, Pennsylvania, was undertaking a strategy to reinvent itself. The leaders decided they needed to eliminate an entire layer of staff, including 125 people. They knew this action could devastate morale and threaten the participation of the remaining staff in the change actions that still lay ahead. But even in a situation as fraught with fear and resentment as this, gaining buy-in from the non-downsized employees proved not only possible but highly effective. A journal article reported:

> Frank disclosure of the downsizing and its purposes by Hamot's leaders, along with ongoing dialogue with employees and the community, averted most of the negative consequences. Since then, Hamot has won recognition in multiple categories as one of the top 100 hospitals in the United States, gained seven percentage points of regional market share, and operated consistently in the black.[2]

Are you buying into buy-in yet?

The process of helping others understand what you want to do in your organization will take time, patience, and planning on your part. Here is some advice for introducing your strategy in a way that gets everybody on your side:

- First, establish the need for having a new strategy. Help the others understand why your company is at a point where it has the opportunity, and even the requirement, to try something different.

- Then present the new strategy clearly and simply. Keep it short, avoiding unnecessary detail and background. Be realistic yet upbeat. Radiate enthusiasm.

- Anticipate questions. After all, upon hearing a new strategy, people will always think, *What does this mean to me?* They may be feeling fear. So invite questions, even push-back, and be receptive and respectful when you get it. Have answers and assurances at the ready.

- As much as seems appropriate, seek input and constructive ideas on the strategy. If people can get their thumbprints on the strategy (at least the execution end of it), it will magically become theirs. Strategy can't be all top-down; this is the bottom-up piece. Put the chalk in the hands of others for the moment.

- Don't get sidetracked by criticism or resistance coming at you. Stay on message. Funnel the conversation toward positive action. Although the strategy may still be in development to some degree, it's a go. And you're leading the advance.

Ask yourself, what would happen to your strategy if something intervened and you couldn't be involved in any of the implementation? Would the people you have passed the strategy on to take it and run with it? Or would the wheels quickly come to a stop?

John Kotter, in his book *Buy-In*, argues, "Our insufficient knowledge about how to get good new ideas accepted by others—a central piece of making anything happen—is becoming more and more of a problem as the world changes faster and faster."[3] Knowing how to gain buy-in, then, is a skill you're going to have to learn as a practitioner of Strategy 3.0.

When you're heading into the uncertainty of a new strategy, it's a great feeling to know your team is lining up at your back.

Disruptions: *No amount of planning or intelligence can predict everything.*

A U.S. manufacturer was hoping to gain a competitive advantage by moving assembly of some of its products to the lower-labor-cost environment of East India. A week before production was set to begin, a monsoon wiped out the factory.

A leading jewelry manufacturer was feeling good about its position and adopted a more-of-the-same policy. But then the leaders were stunned when they started losing share to an upstart company that was marketing jewelry through new channels such as wine bars, sporting events, and college sororities.

A small independent film company invested its borrowed capital in a movie with a story topic no one had ever seen on the big screen before. Then they found out from *Variety* that a Hollywood company with far deeper pockets was coming out with a similar movie at almost the same time.

Disruptions.

They happen in all areas of life. They happen in business too, no matter how careful you are.

If you think you can roll out your strategy without the unexpected sooner or later impinging on it, you're not living in the real world.

Disruptions can be devastating or merely frustrating. They can be long lasting or temporary in their influence. They can come from inside or outside the organization. But one way or another, they *will* come.

You can be the smartest person alive, and have the best thought-out strategy ever, but you're still vulnerable to disruption. Why? Because you're not in control of everything. None of us is. Here is a sampling of areas that regularly hand out I-didn't-see-it-coming surprises:

- *People's health.* What if the visionary founder starts showing signs of dementia?
- *Macro economics and markets.* Not even Warren Buffett has more than a minuscule influence over these. We can only react.
- *Weather.* It's tough to be an outdoor wedding organizer in the middle of the rainiest June in decades.

- *Accidents, production mistakes, and plain old bad luck.* Pulping the entire print run of a book with a misspelled title on the cover is going to further slim an already anorexic profit margin.
- *Competitors.* This is a big one—and the main reason that disruption is becoming more and more common these days. There are others out there who are deliberately trying to alter the playing field under your feet. One article said, "Disruptive innovations are like missiles launched at your business."[4] And in fact, because there is so much innovation in the world today, a pervasive entrepreneurial spirit, and social media at our fingertips, the time lag to learn and try is practically nothing. Somebody else can disrupt your strategy, or at least a part of it, overnight. Are you scared yet?

The solution to disruption is not to become fearful or fatalistic. You can, and should, keep planning. You can, and should, keep looking for ways to minimize risk. But at the same time, stay alert to what's going on all around you. And make sure your strategy is flexible enough to allow you to do some improvising when the unanticipated shows up at the door.

And remember, disruption is not all bad. If you're

"MAKE SURE YOUR STRATEGY IS FLEXIBLE ENOUGH TO ALLOW YOU TO DO SOME IMPROVISING WHEN THE UNANTICIPATED SHOWS UP AT THE DOOR."

smart enough, fast enough, and agile enough, maybe you can find a way to take the new reality that has been sprung on you and turn it to your advantage.

Execution: *Not even the best strategic plan self-executes.*

Parenting is much more than just deciding with your spouse that you want to have a child and going through the fun part of producing the tyke. When you leave the hospital with your bundle, you realize you're going to have to guide and raise a real-live human being for years to come.

Likewise, strategy is much more than just planning what your organization will do next. You also have to make it happen over a period of time—effectively and cost efficiently, so that you achieve your purpose.

What we're talking about here is *execution:* getting things done. Execution is not some separate, lesser phase, subsumed under tactics rather than strategy. Execution is a part of strategy.

Lawrence G. Hrebiniak, author of *Making Strategy Work*, said,

> When companies separate the planning and doing—that's wrong. Executive strategy requires ownership at all levels, from corporate level managers on down.

Strategic success really demands a simultaneous view of planning and doing. The greater the overlap of doers and planners, the greater probability of success.[5]

I would suggest that good execution is actually more important in the Strategy 3.0 world than in the world that is passing. You see, the flip side of the fact that fast innovation has become so widespread is that ideas are a dime a dozen. Good execution can set you apart from a competitor who's spinning out game-changing concepts but doesn't know how to turn them into winning products or services.

In the latest edition of their classic book on execution, Larry Bossidy and Ram Charan point out that, as competition becomes fiercer, the ability to execute can become the factor that determines who survives. They argue that leaders need to link the three central factors of people, strategy, and operations to build a company based on dialogue, intellectual honesty, and realism.[6]

Business performance consultant Ed Barrows reported on how Prescolite and Progress Lighting—two brands of Connecticut-based Hubbell Incorporated—merged strategy and execution.

They created a process that incorporates both strategy formulation activities, such as ongoing analysis of changes in market conditions, with execution activities such as management of integrated strategic programs. At the start of the planning year, they perform a "deep dive" on critical competitive issues facing the businesses. The remainder of the year they focus on measuring and monitoring the progress they are making. They also keep a running list of "must-do" integrated programs that they readjust as business conditions change.[7]

Consider these keys to successful execution that I have observed along the way:

+ Understand your internal resources (people, money, capacity, and so on).
+ Establish clear, reachable goals.
+ Communicate and over-communicate with everyone involved.
+ Establish role clarity and set up swim lanes for people and activities.
+ Make sure the folks doing the execution buy-in to what must be done.
+ Empower people to do their jobs.

- Provide top-down support and be ready to clear roadblocks and hurdles.
- Measure results.

The authors of a *Harvard Business Review* article on execution said, "A brilliant strategy, blockbuster product, or breakthrough technology can put you on the competitive map, but only solid execution can keep you there. You have to be able to deliver on your intent."[8]

Execution is at a premium in today's world. You can't just give birth to a great idea. You also have to nurture it to maturity.

Fast: *Speed wins (usually).*

In 1884, German inventor Paul Nipkow patented the "Nipkow disc," a device able to divide a picture into a mosaic of points and lines. It was the essential scanning method needed for video transmission and thus has earned Nipkow the sobriquet "the father of television." The patent lapsed fifteen years later for lack of interest.

The earliest commercially produced television sets came onto the market in 1928. By 1942, when production was temporarily halted for war reasons, fewer than nine thousand sets had been purchased in the United States. Television use finally skyrocketed in the late 1940s and early 1950s when the prices for television sets dropped and programming improved. (Not that Milton Berle in a dress was really all that funny.)

Seven decades passed from the invention of the Nipkow disc until television use in American households tipped the 50 percent mark.

Slow used to be the way.

Fast is how it goes now.

Twitter went from concept to worldwide sensation in four years.

Within a week after the release of a new video game, the maker may have already made up to 70 percent of the profit it will ever get off the game.

Apple's real-time supply chain delivers iPads from Shenzhen, China, to Palo Alto in four days.

Pekka Ala-Pietila, a board member of the Finnish tech company Nokia, said, "Five to 10 years ago you would set your vision and strategy and then start following it. That does not work any more.

Now you have to be alert every day, week and month to renew your strategy."[9]

But it's not simply a matter of making decisions quick, quick, quick. For example, increasing operational speed can reduce product quality. Rather, what makes a company fast and good is establishing a culture of flexibility and agility where leaders see a critical problem or opportunity right away, take enough time to make the right decision (but no more than enough time), and then act on it immediately.

In short, velocity matters. But so does vector. Researchers in one study said this:

> Higher-performing companies with strategic speed made alignment a priority. They became more open to ideas and discussion. They encouraged innovative thinking. And they allowed time to reflect and learn. By contrast, performance suffered at firms that moved fast all the time, focused too much on maximizing efficiency, stuck to tested methods, didn't foster employee collaboration, and weren't overly concerned about alignment.[10]

Speed doesn't guarantee success. You can be fast and still fail.

But one thing can be said for sure: being slow will cause you to fall behind in today's fast-paced world.

Learn to enact your current strategy…and the next one…and the next one—*fast*.

Imperfections: *Every strategy, even one of the really good ones, is flawed and requires compromise.*

Business consultant Stuart Cross tells the story of working with a retail company whose leaders considered an idea to target a new group of customers through a nonretail channel. Modeling suggested that this strategy could net up to 50 percent top-line growth in sales. The problem? The same modeling showed that the profit margins in this new activity would be only half that of retail sales. This was enough to deflate the executives' interest in the strategy. Better to stick with a type of sales they understood better and could wring a fatter margin out of, they reasoned. It took one brave and far-seeing manager a full year of negotiations with his higher-ups to convince them that they should devote resources to the nonretail channel and figure out how to increase margins along the way.[11]

This was a company that was ready to forgo a huge opportunity because a proposed strategy was imperfect.

Others, by contrast, accept imperfection and move ahead anyway.

Before becoming mayor of New York City, Michael Bloomberg built up a financial information and media empire. Looking back in 2001, he identified one key to his success as being his company's willingness to put a good strategy into action quickly without insisting that it be perfect first.

> We made mistakes of course. Most of them were omissions we didn't think of when we initially wrote the software. We fixed them by doing it over and over, again and again. We do the same today. While our competitors are still sucking their thumbs trying to make the design perfect, we're already on prototype version No. 5. By the time our rivals are ready with wires and screws, we are on version No. 10. It gets back to planning versus acting. We act from day one; others plan how to plan—for months.[12]

No matter how much you love a strategy you've come up with, don't make the mistake of thinking it is perfect. It isn't. You can't foresee everything.

Of course, you shouldn't proceed with a strategy that is so badly flawed that it's unworkable. Don't short-circuit your own progress by planning poorly. You need to take the commonsense steps of doing rigorous analysis, avoiding overconfidence, and so on.[13]

But if the strategy has strong potential, despite some weaknesses or unknowns, learn to live with the flaws until you can compensate for them later. Trust in your speed and adaptability to enable you to invent the future on the fly.

I love how one tech blogger argued that it's better to get a product to market than to dawdle over making improvements.

> Your company, product, service or application will never be finished. It will never be what you would consider to be "perfect." Unfortunately, many entrepreneurs don't get this concept. They lock themselves away in dark rooms and keep tweaking and tinkering, thinking that if they can just get everything perfect, their business will be a success.

"NO MATTER HOW MUCH YOU LOVE A STRATEGY YOU'VE COME UP WITH, DON'T MAKE THE MISTAKE OF THINKING IT IS PERFECT. IT ISN'T. YOU CAN'T FORESEE EVERYTHING."

In the meantime, those companies that simply launch their offering gain a major advantage. While they wouldn't launch something half-finished they realize that 90 percent perfect is "good enough." They understand that there's really no way to know every flaw, bug or feature request until they actually get their product in the hands of their intended customer.[14]

Let "good enough" be good enough for your organization. Don't swallow the opportunity cost that comes from squelching a promising, though imperfect, strategy.

Momentum: *A flywheel can propel you or it can break you.*

When you move to implement your strategy, things are going to start happening quickly. Your employees will be busy. Plans will unfold. Like switched-on machinery, your organization will hum with new activity.

It's easy to get excited at this point. The plan is becoming a reality! Momentum is building!

But this is when you've got to contain your enthusiasm and evaluate the nature of the momentum. Because you see, momentum can move in the right direction or it can move in the wrong direction.

In his classic book *Good to Great*, Jim Collins describes the Flywheel Effect and its evil twin, the Doom Loop.[15]

According to Collins, a company is like a big, heavy flywheel. It takes steady, repetitive pushing in the right direction, over a period of time, to get the rotational momentum you want. But when that big flywheel is spinning freely like a planet in space, it's a beautiful thing. It throws off tremendous output. Collins describes it in terms of a breakthrough:

> With each turn, it moves faster, and then—at some point, you can't say exactly when—you break through. The momentum of the heavy wheel kicks in your favor. It spins faster and faster, with its own weight propelling it. You aren't pushing any harder, but the flywheel is accelerating, its momentum building, its speed increasing.[16]

I like to think of it this way: Success breeds support and commitment, which breeds even greater success, which breeds more support and commitment.... Around and around the flywheel goes. People like to support winners and efforts that win!

Here's where high-level success over an extended period of time appears. When a company breaks away from the pack with sustained rapid growth, or when a nonprofit gets wide notice for exceptional service to its mission, you know the Flywheel Effect is in place.

But on the other hand, an organization that lurches back and forth, failing to make wise and disciplined contributions to its goals over time, creates another kind of pattern. If you see an organization that is selling off assets to stay alive, or is desperately trying to recover the lost reputation of its brand, you know it's stuck in a Doom Loop. Collins, again, says:

> Disappointing results lead to reaction without understanding, which leads to a new direction—a new leader, a new program—which leads to no momentum, which leads to disappointing results. It's a steady, downward spiral. Those who have experienced a Doom Loop know how it drains the spirit right out of a company.[17]

And this is why, early on in your strategy, you've got to ask yourself in which direction the momentum of your organization is running. Get good-quality, objective feedback. Then, if the feedback tells a cautionary tale, have the courage to halt your current momentum quickly by pausing, pivoting, or pulling the plug on your strategy.

You must intervene if a Doom Loop is in the making within your organization. But even more importantly, make the creation of *positive* momentum a meta-goal of your leadership. You'll know that you've succeeded historically as a leader if the flywheel is operating and your organization is spinning with coordinated activity and extraordinary productivity.

Progression: *Advancement is about taking multiple steps, not making one genius move.*

Business scholar John Kotter examined more than one hundred companies that were trying to adapt to increasingly challenging competition. What did he discover?

"The most general lesson to be learned from the more successful cases," he reported, "is that the change process goes through a series of phases that, in total, usually require a considerable length of time. Skipping steps creates only the illusion of speed and never produces a satisfying result."[18]

Jim Collins, similarly, has shown that successful companies undertake a "20 Mile March" of methodical steps toward their goal, not a sprint to the finish line.[19]

In chess, you don't get to checkmate until you clear away some pieces and follow a precogitated sequence to pin your opponent's king.

Most baseball games are won on the strength of base hits and steals, not home runs.

My point in all of this is that, much as we'd like to think there is a silver bullet in strategy, there really isn't. One genius move won't give you success. You have to get there one step at a time.

This is actually good news, since most of us aren't geniuses anyway. Victory, it turns out, goes to the merely canny who work hard and never give up.

Yes, you have to move fast in Strategy 3.0. But you also have to expect to keep moving. You move fast again and again. This means that, along with agility and adaptability, you need some old-fashioned virtues like patience, discipline, and determination.

Of course, not all moves in organizational leadership are equal. Some are more important than others, even extremely important. So I am not saying that a single insight can't lift a company above others or force a new trajectory. But to take one insight all the way to its fully leveraged end might involve dozens of moves, not just one.

Since this is the case, you need to build muscle into your organization. Model perseverance and a savvy go-get-'em attitude. Don't get too excited about any good outcome or too discouraged about any bad result. Sure, there are incredible things to celebrate and serious setbacks to overcome, but don't be a leader who is always at one extreme or the other. Learn to live in the middle. Advance, assess, repeat.

When your organization gets to where you had hoped it would go—or maybe even someplace better—you'll look like a genius.

Sequencing: *Sorting the order is often harder than getting the clarity.*

If getting the order right didn't matter, air traffic controllers wouldn't be concerned about which airplane landed when. If getting the order right didn't matter, baseball managers wouldn't care who hit in the clean-up spot and who hit ninth. If getting the order right didn't matter, the chef wouldn't pay attention to when he put the dishes in the oven so that they all arrive at your table hot.

You get the picture. Order *does* matter.

In organizational strategy, order is one of the often-overlooked qualities that can spell the difference between a W and an L. Strategic sequencing is simply the arranging of items in a specific order for a specific purpose—what goes first, second, third, and so on.

The purpose of good sequencing is to gain an advantage. This advantage can be to build on prior momentum. It can be to get off to a fast start. It can be to get harnessed into the larger stampede of events.

The owner of a restaurant in New Orleans should realize that the upcoming Mardi Gras period is going to mean a spike in reservations.

She'll be wise to keep the carnival season in mind as she plans the timing of such things as rolling out a new promotion, updating the website, hiring additional staff, ordering supplies, scheduling vacations, and more. None of this minor. If she gets the timing or the order wrong on one or more of these items, it could turn Fat Tuesday into Skinny Tuesday for her business.

- Sequencing the steps of your strategy well can *make your operation more efficient*. What happens if the two-by-fours haven't shown up at the building site when the framers are ready to swing a hammer?

- Sequencing can *maintain productivity*. If the TSA isn't staffing the checkpoints properly for peak travel times, your security line is going to stretch all the way back to the Cinnabon shop.

- Sequencing can anticipate *if-this-then-that outcomes*. A city planning team tasked with rejuvenating downtown might choose to focus first on upgrading the shopping district and only later expand the public transit system to handle the increased load of travelers.

To sequence well, step back and take a wide-angle view of your business or nonprofit. Identify the needle-moving choices that trigger other choices. Don't forget that pausing can be one part of your sequencing order that can help align you with smart timing. As with any other part of strategy, stay flexible and revise as you go.

Getting clarity on what you want to do is crucial for your strategy. But setting the parts of your strategy into motion at the right time and in the right order may be even more crucial. Don't overlook it.

Singularity: *Few companies can execute more than one strategy at a time no matter what they put on paper.*

Organizations are complex, and the bigger they are, the more complex they are, doing many different things all at once—right?

My answer is that this is true only in one sense. If you look at the details of an organization—the many people who are a part of it and the tasks and projects they are carrying out—then, yes, it is complex. A lot of different things are happening.

But if you step back and assess the overall thrust of the organization, you will notice that it is actually doing only one thing. To put it another way, it probably has just one strategic driver. In this sense, it's simple rather than complex. (Or at least it is if it's an effective organization.)

Surprising?

Think of a pointillist painting, such as Georges Seurat's famous "A Sunday Afternoon on the Island of La Grand Jatte." You know, the one with Parisians standing or reclining on the banks of a park lake, some of the women with parasols. A pointillist painting like this is made up of thousands of small dots of color. Stand close, and all you see are the dots. Stand back, and you take in a unified scene.

That's the way it is with strategy. An organization can effectively carry out only one master strategy at a time. And it would be a mistake to try to do otherwise.

What brought down the banking industry in the collapse of 2008–09? One reason may have been that banks were trying to do too much, dabbling in ill-advised mortgages when they should have stuck to core banking.[20]

A jet takes off heading for just one destination. Getting it there involves many steps and processes, but success is landing safely and on time at the airport identified in the flight plan.

I have a client who has the goal to double his business within two years. If I were to advise him to simultaneously pursue a strategy to stockpile cash, it would be a disaster. Growth requires investment of cash. He needs to focus on his double-in-two strategy for now. A cash pileup will come later.

It can be tempting to try to carry out more than one major strategy at a time. You can put multiple strategies on paper and order that they be carried out. But it just won't work. You'll likely get confusion in the ranks and a diffusion of resources, and you won't see your organization moving ahead.

There's genius in the simple clarity of having one big goal. So, while others in the organization are carrying out their multitudinous projects, the people at the top have got to keep a singular focus in view. Later they'll have another strategy. But for now, they need to focus on the one they've got.

To succeed in strategy, get simple.

"TO SUCCEED IN STRATEGY, GET SIMPLE."

Spotlighting: *Focus your best assets on fixing your weakest link.*

In your organization, where should you deploy your best assets and pump in the most energy?

In answering that question, many leaders would say that they would try to maximize what's working best for them. For example, if a personal products company has launched a new line and the early sales are indicating great promise of profit, the leaders might pile on the sales resources to go for a big win.

And that kind of deployment of resources *might* be the best choice.

Unless there's a problem somewhere in the system that's serious enough to cripple the strategy.

Let's say the distribution system that the personal products company uses is inadequate for handling larger volume. In that case, the whole strategy of growth is at risk. The smart move would be to throw in the talent that's needed to fix the distribution problem first...and *then* double down on sales promotion.

It's like having a water hose with a hole on it. Sure, you can crank up the water volume if you want, but it will only make the leak worse—and it might even ruin the hose. Patch the hole, then turn up the water.

I call identifying and going after significant problems *spotlighting*. You shine the bright light of your attention on your whole system until you find the weakest link and then you take steps to reverse the problem.

Why is spotlighting a valuable skill for a 3.0 strategist to have? Because your strategy can never move faster than the piece of the system that is lagging behind. And because you can never be more efficient in execution than your clunkiest process. Every real solution is part of a bigger ecosystem.

Dwayne Spradlin, CEO of a problem solving company, described the necessity of taking problems seriously and dealing with them quickly if you want your strategy to succeed. Here's the scenario he outlined:

Someone in the bowels of the organization is assigned to fix a very specific, near-term problem.

But because the firm doesn't employ a rigorous process for understanding the dimensions of the problem, leaders miss an opportunity to address underlying strategic issues.... Organizational teams speed toward a solution, fearing that if they spend too much time defining the problem, their superiors will punish them for taking so long to get to the starting line.

Ironically, that approach is more likely to waste time and money and reduce the odds of success than one that strives at the outset to achieve an in-depth understanding of the problem and its importance to the firm.[21]

Where do you need to shine the spotlight so that your organization can open up the bottleneck that's threatening to choke off the success of your strategy? Like Sherlock Holmes, sniff out clues and track down internal risks within your business or nonprofit. Like the Mission Control team assigned to Apollo 13, jump into action as soon as you hear "Houston, we've got a problem."

Put your best talent on your hardest problem and clear it away fast so that your strategy can move full speed ahead.

Structure: Every good idea must settle into a container to reach its optimal value.

The idea that can serve as the seed of your next great strategy can come from almost anywhere. You notice an unmet need out there in the world and start wondering how you could fill the gap. While you're taking a shower or running on the treadmill, your subconscious is humming away. You happen to talk to someone who's offbeat, or visit someplace that's off the beaten path, and it explodes an *Aha!* in your brain.

You're on your way!

Or at least it seems that way.

Idea generation is crucial. *But it doesn't mean a thing if you don't do something constructive with the great idea the universe hands you.*

Let me put it another way. For a while, it is fine for ideas to simply float around. But an idea that just moves from happy hour to happy hour, or from brainstorming session to brainstorming session, never roots and develops. You need a container for it.

A seed without a pot or a plot of ground to germinate in won't grow.

With all I've said so far about vision and creativity and shaking things up as an organizational strategist, it might seem as if I've stigmatized seemingly stiff and boring words such as *structure* and *framework*. But the truth is, while there's no effective strategy these days without intuitive leaps of insight, there does come a time when you've got to pour the concrete into a form if you're ever going to make a foundation out of it.

At the right time, structure isn't bad. It's good. Strategy 3.0 is fast but not formless.

The container or structure you need might take many forms:

+ It might be the *overall organizational* form you use. For example, if you and a friend are passionate about helping the hungry in your city, you might choose to create a nonprofit as the structure to help you feed the poor.
+ In a larger organization, it might be the *articulated plan or strategy map* you're using for a new venture. An example would be the action plan you put together based on discussions you had at your latest executive retreat.

- It might be the *team or group* that is leading the strategy. Think of an acquisition team that leads the effort to buy another company.

The form can vary. And not every framework has to be rigid or strict. But every strategy needs some kind of structure if it's going to go anywhere.

Here's something I've observed. Just as certain people seem to naturally fit best in certain types of companies (a hair-on-fire start-up situation, for example, instead of a more straitlaced major corporation), so different strategies naturally fit best within certain types of structures. A part of your role as a leader, then, is to match strategy to structure wisely.

What are you trying to achieve with your amazing new idea? What form will give the best shape to the idea and produce the outcome you want?

Don't despise structure. Use structure. For only when you have structure in place can you test the operational viability of your plan, estimate your people needs, get an accurate idea of costs, gauge the true returns you can expect, and see what else still needs to be done. Only through structure can you get anything done.

Put your strategy in a container and thrive.

Talent: *A great hire will outlive a great plan every time.*

In the bygone Strategy 2.0 world, five-year business plans were the norm. Now that 3.0 is upon us, strategy cycles are getting shorter and shorter. One implication of this is that your employees are going to be around longer than your current strategy. Will they serve you well, not just for what you're up to right now, but also for the strategies yet to come?

With the *what* of your business changing faster and faster, the who becomes more important than ever. I'd go so far as to say that the war for great talent is more fierce than the battle for great ideas. The human element is the most valuable element.

Every two years, IBM carries out a massive survey of CEOs to see what's happening in business, globally. What do you suppose was the number-one theme that emerged from the CEOs who responded to the 2012 survey?

If you imagined it was the impact of technology or social media, you'd be wrong. It was the importance of how these leaders treated their people. Top executives are focused on tapping the ability of workers to help their companies adapt to new realities.

"CEOs have a strategy in the unending war for talent," the study says. "They are creating more open and collaborative cultures—encouraging employees to connect, learn from each other and thrive in a world of rapid change."[22] The insight underlying this emphasis is that the people within the company are of crucial importance.

All strategy comes to life on the stage of humanity. In other words, it takes people to take the risks, to make the decisions, to get things done, and to problem-solve when the strategy hits a hurdle, goes sideways, or is disrupted by new realities. This means that, over time, it is the great hire who will help shape or implement any strategic plan.

Many things have been written about how to hire well—network, advertise broadly, and so on. This conventional advice is fine as far as it goes. But I want to focus on a few principles you may not have heard anywhere else.

- *Hire a B+ candidate.* Sometimes leaders will hire someone who is insanely capable in one area but abysmal in another, and they regret it when the area of weakness starts making life miserable for many in the organization. That's why I suggest hiring someone who earns a composite B+ in the three core areas of chemistry (getting along with the rest of your team), competence (ability to fulfill their role on the job), and character (being someone you can rely on). Obviously, if you *can* find someone who earns an A in all three areas, that's even better. But don't hold out for it unnecessarily. Grab a composite B+ worker if you can find one—you'll have someone on board who will serve you superbly as you roll out your strategies over time.

- *Hire slow, fire fast.* Unfortunately, many leaders get this one backward—and then find themselves stuck with trying to execute a strategy with the wrong players on the bench. I know you're busy. Nevertheless, when hiring, it's incredibly important that you take all the time and go through all the steps you need to be confident that you have the right person. You're far less likely to make a mistake that way.

If you do, correct it quickly by getting rid of the misplaced employee. Having the right crew on board is that important.

+ *Keep on "hiring" after you hire.* Too many companies woo great talent before they bring the newcomer in…and then almost immediately start taking the new hire for granted. In this way they neutralize their own hard work. Instead of that foolishness, continue showing you care about this person by investing in his or her professional development. Keep your employee motivated, empowered, and giving of her or his best. (That's what the CEOs in the IBM study were trying to do.) It's like keeping the romance alive in a marriage: continue wooing a great hire to create longevity in the relationship.

As you're looking toward your new strategy, remember that it's crucial to have the right talent to get things done.

Learning to hire brilliantly may, in fact, turn out to be your most important strategy.

Tension: *Change seldom happens without friction.*

Establishing a new strategy is going to introduce changes all over your organization. It's going to dislodge people from their routines and likely recombine some of them in different working teams. It's going to pose new questions and expose new zones of uncertainty. A natural result of all this is the creation of hot spots of tension among some of your employees.

But here's the thing about tension…

Some tension is destructive and some tension is constructive.

The first kind of hot spot—destructive tension—you want to put out with a hose as soon as it crops up. The second kind—constructive tension—you're better off letting burn for a while, because this kind of tension can actually become a part of your execution of the strategy.

Are you prepared to accept constructive tension within your organization?

An old proverb says, "Iron sharpens iron." In my experience, though, many people would prefer to sharpen iron with something softer, if they could.

The heat and sparks that are created when two people grate upon each other in disagreement make them uncomfortable. But if you want an edge on your blade, sharpen your iron with iron.

William Wrigley Jr., a businessman whose name lives on in chewing gum and the Chicago Cubs' ballpark, used to say, "If two people in business always agree, one of them is unnecessary."[23] Learn to see debate and opposing points of view as important steps on the way to a new synthesis of agreement and action.

But of course you want the tension to be about the right things. If two people are at each other's throats over the colors to be used in a new print ad campaign, that could be a waste of time and emotional capital. Better to have debates about big ideas. Are we going to expand into China? Is it time for an IPO?

The company leadership should set the ground rules for optimizing tension and guiding employees through conflict. Consider these commonsense approaches:

- Work on creating a reservoir of trust among the team members or partners.
- Teach people to become comfortable with honesty and directness.

- Don't let employees use e-mail or social media to advance a disagreement. They should talk it out in person.
- Insist that they keep the debate focused on work issues. They should never let the conversation slide into personality issues.
- Assign someone to be the facilitator of a discussion or the blender of diverse views.
- Let the tension play out long enough but not too long.

Wildfire is one of nature's ways of renewing the landscape. Without letting the fire of disagreement get out of control in your organization, learn to use it to the advantage of your strategy.

Winning: *Luck is not predictable advantage.*

A. G. Lafley, CEO of Procter & Gamble, gives businesspeople this simple but crucial piece of advice: "Play to win, rather than simply to compete."[24] Your strategy might be interesting and engrossing for its own sake. But never forget that its purpose is to achieve something substantial for your organization.

You might be intending to start a business, land a new account, increase market share, acquire "mind share," double your donor base, or something else. But whatever your goal is, keep it before you and go after it with all the healthy competitiveness hidden inside you. Deploy your strategy to win.

Obvious?

Well, it is. But do you know what? I've noticed something disturbing in many leaders. They think they are playing to win, but they aren't. They're really hoping in luck. Unconsciously, they think becoming successful depends on being fortunate, perhaps with a product introduction that strikes the public's fancy at just the right moment, a marketing campaign that happens to go viral, or something else.

Of course, there is an element of luck in business, since some factors are out of our control. So if you win once, that may be luck. Learning to capitalize on the good luck that comes your way can be a useful part of your operating procedure.[25] But remember, luck isn't something you can rely on. It isn't a competitive advantage in itself. Having a great plan or strategy and working it with all your might—*that's* a competitive advantage.

I've never been on a flight where the pilot filed luck as part of the flight plan. Instead, the pilot relies on his training, equipment, and systems. He navigates the weather, balancing fuel and weight. He keeps in constant communication with those who can help him and sticks to the flight plan. He's got a strategy to "win"—to get the plane to the arrival airport—and he's relying on that strategy instead of on luck. And I, for one, am very glad about that.

I remember years ago spending an afternoon with John Wooden, the legendary basketball coach who led the UCLA basketball team to ten championships in twelve years. He said, "The importance of repetition until automaticity cannot be overstated."

In sports as in business, you repeat your skills again and again to hone your ability and produce a record of sustained winning. You don't trust in luck. You advance your strategy. Sure, there is always an element of luck involved in certain sporting events. But good coaches don't plan on it.

A smart, comprehensive strategy, pursued nimbly yet resolutely, will create a pattern of success even in the fluid 3.0 world in which we live. Lafley said, "Maybe not right away, but eventually companies without winning strategies die. A great invention or product idea can create a company, build value, and win in the marketplace for a while. But to last, the company behind the idea must…sustain lasting competitive advantage."[26]

As much as possible, leave nothing to chance. Get your best strategy into place and execute it like an athlete for whom second place is never good enough. And if luck happens to lend a hand—so much the better!

NOTES

CHAPTER 2

1. "You Choose," *The Economist*, December 16, 2010, http://www.economist.com/node/17723028.1

2. See Chris Anderson, *The Long Tail: Why the Future of Business Is Selling Less of More*, rev. ed. (New York: Hyperion, 2008); and Chris Anderson, *Free: How Today's Smartest Businesses Profit by Giving Something for Nothing*, rev. ed. (New York: Hyperion, 2010).

3. Grant McCracken, "The Corporation Is at Odds with the Future," May 29, 2013, HBR Blog Network, http://blogs.hbr.org/cs/2013/05/the_corp_is_odds_future.html.

4. Quoted in Dana O'Donovan and Noah Rimland Flower, "The Strategic Plan Is Dead. Long Live Strategy," *w*, January 10, 2013, http://www.ssireview.org/blog/entry/the_strategic_plan_is_dead._long_live_strategy.

5. Read their story in Walter Kiechel, *The Lords of Strategy: The Secret Intellectual History of the New Corporate World* (Boston: Harvard Business Press, 2010).

6. "Capitalizing on Complexity: Insights from the Global Chief Executive Officer Study," IBM,

http://www-304.ibm.com/businesscenter/cpe/download0/200422/ceostudy_2010.pdf

7. O'Donovan and Flower, "The Strategic Plan Is Dead."

8. Quoted in Jocelyn R. Davis, Henry M. Frechette Jr., and Edwin H. Boswell, *Strategic Speed: Mobilize People, Accelerate Execution* (Boston: Harvard Business Review Press, 2010), 20.

9. Martin Reeves and Mike Deimler, "Adaptability: The New Competitive Advantage," *Harvard Business Review*, July 2011, http://hbr.org/2011/07/adaptability-the-new-competitive-advantage.

10. Martin Reeves, "Know Which Strategy Style Is Right for Your Organization," HBR Blog Network, September 12, 2012, http://blogs.hbr.org/cs/2012/09/know_which_strategy_style_is.html.

CHAPTER 3

1. The five stages are as follows: (1) hubris born of success, (2) undisciplined pursuit of more, (3) denial of risk and peril, (4) grasping for salvation, and (5) capitulation to irrelevance or

death. See Jim Collins, *How the Mighty Have Fallen: And Why Some Companies Never Give In* (Jim Collins, 2009).

2. Peter Guber, *Tell to Win: Connect, Persuade, and Triumph with the Hidden Power of Story* (New York: Crown, 2011).

3. Steve Denning, "The Science of Storytelling," *Forbes*, March 9, 2012, http://www.forbes.com/sites/stevedenning/2012/03/09/the-science-of-storytelling/.

4. For a book that unites the right brain of "Aha!" with the left brain of "Get to work," see Steven G. Blank, *The Four Steps to the Epiphany: Successful Strategies for Products That Win*, 3rd ed. (S. G. Blank, 2007).

5. Michael V. Copeland, "Intel's Cultural Anthopologist," *Fortune*, September 30, 2011, http://money.cnn.com/2010/09/20/technology/intel_anthropologist.fortune/index.htm.

6. SWOT, the time-tested planning matrix, stands for Strengths, Weaknesses, Opportunities, and Threats.

7. Jim Collins and Morten T. Hansen, *Great by Choice: Uncertainty, Chaos, and Luck—Why*

Some Thrive Despite Them All (New York: Harper Business, 2011), 1.

8. If you want to learn to make better choices, I recommend reading Chip Heath and Dan Heath, *Decisive: How to Make Better Choices in Life and Work* (New York: Crown, 2013).

9. Eliyahu Federman, "Why Businesses Should Embrace Negative Customer Feedback," *Social Media Today*, May 1, 2013, http://socialmediatoday.com/elifederman/1417061/why-businesses-should-embrace-negative-customer-feedback.

10. To see how Eric Ries, author of *The Lean Startup*, coined the term *pivot*, watch the video at http://www.fastcompany.com/1836238/how-eric-ries-coined-pivot-and-what-your-business-can-learn-it.

11. J.C. Penney, "Come Back to See Us" commercial, YouTube, https://www.youtube.com/watch?v=I8qhJOfNfso.

12. Adam L. Penenberg, "Enter the Pivot: The Critical Course Corrections of Flickr, Fab.com, and More," *Fast Company*, May 2, 2012, http://www.fastcompany.com/1834196/enter-pivot-critical-course-corrections-flickr-

fabcom-and-more.

13. Robert Safian, "Letter from the Editor: The Adrien Brody Rule," *Fast Company*, February 2012, http://www.fastcompany.com/1802659/letter-editor-adrien-brody-rule.

14. For help in making a choice, see Seth Godin, *The Dip: A Little Book That Teaches You When to Quit* (and When to Stick) (New York: Penguin, 2007).

15. Karl Stark and Bill Stewart, "Are You Doubling Down for Growth?" *Inc.*, January 27, 2012, http://www.inc.com/karl-and-bill/are-you-doubling-down-for-growth.html.

CHAPTER 4

1. This and the other examples of strategic failures listed here are cited in Paul B. Carroll and Chunka Mui, *Billion-Dollar Lessons: What You Can Learn from the Most Inexcusable Business Failures of the Last 25 Years* (New York: Portfolio, 2008).

2. Charles Roxburgh, "Hidden Flaws in Strategy," *McKinsey Quarterly*, May 2003, http://www.

mckinsey.com/insights/strategy/hidden_
flaws_in_strategy.

CHAPTER 5

1. Karl Moore and Brian McGowan, "Agility:
   The Ingredient That Will Define Next
   Generation Leadership," *Forbes*, June 12,
   2012, http://www.forbes.com/sites/
   karlmoore/2012/06/12/agility-the-
   ingredient-that-will-define-next-generation-
   leadership/.

2. *Harvard Management Update*, "How to Win
   the Buy-in: Setting the Stage for Change,"
   HBR Blog Network, February 26, 2008,
   http://blogs.hbr.org/hmu/2008/02/how-to-
   win-the-buyin-setting-t-1.html.

3. John P. Kotter and Lorne A. Whitehead, *Buy-
   In: Saving Your Good Idea from Getting Shot
   Down* (Boston: Harvard Review Press, 2010),
   13.

4. Maxwell Wessel and Clayton M. Christensen,
   "Surviving Disruption," *Harvard Business
   Review*, December 2012, http://hbr.
   org/2012/12/surviving-disruption.

5. Quoted in "Got a good strategy? Now try to

implement it," interview with Lawrence G. Hrebiniak, *Knowledge@Wharton*, April 6, 2005, http://knowledge.wharton.upenn.edu/article.cfm?articleid=1173. See also Lawrence G. Hrebiniak, *Making Strategy Work: Leading Effective Execution and Change*, 2nd edition (Upper Saddle River, NJ: FT Press, 2013).

6. Larry Bossidy and Ram Charan, *Execution: The Discipline of Getting Things Done*, updated edition (New York: Random House, 2011).

7. Ed Barrows, "Four Fatal Flaws of Strategic Planning," HBR Blog Network, March 13, 2009, http://blogs.hbr.org/hmu/2009/03/four-fatal-flaws-of-strategic.html.

8. Gary L. Neilsen, Karla L. Martin, and Elizabeth Powers, "The Secrets to Successful Strategy Execution," *Harvard Business Review*, June 2008, http://hbr.org/2008/06/the-secrets-to-successful-strategy-execution/.

9. Quoted in David Ibison, "A Discreet but Potent Influence," *Financial Times*, December 4, 2006, http://www.ft.com/intl/cms/s/0/dedd0e6c-833b-11db-a38a-0000779e2340.html#axzz2c4Q8rpfH.

10. Jocelyn R. Davis and Tom Atkinson, "Need

speed? Slow down," *Harvard Business Review*, May 2010, http://hbr.org/2010/05/need-speed-slow-down/ar/1.

11. Stuart Cross, *The CEO's Strategy Handbook: How to Create, Sustain, and Accelerate Profit Growth* (Hawkhurst Cranbrook, Kent, UK: Global Professional Publishing, 2011), 30–31.

12. Michael Bloomberg, *Bloomberg by Bloomberg* (New York: Wiley, 2001), 52.

13. See Barrows, "Four Fatal Flaws,"; and Charles Roxburgh, "Hidden Flaws in Strategy," *McKinsey Quarterly*, May 2003, http://www.mckinsey.com/insights/strategy/hidden_flaws_in_strategy.

14. Luc Segers, "Find Out Why Speed Wins Over Perfection in Business," *Equalminds*, July 11, 2013, http://www.equalminds.be/speed-over-perfection/.

15. Jim Collins, *Good to Great: Why Some Companies Make the Leap...and Others Don't* (New York: HarperCollins, 2001), Chapter 8.

16. Jim Collins, "Good to Great," October 2001, http://www.jimcollins.com/article_topics/articles/good-to-great.html.

17. Ibid.

18. John P. Kotter, "Leading Change: Why Transformation Efforts Fail," Harvard Business Review, January 2007 (originally published in 1995), http://hbr.org/2007/01/leading-change-why-transformation-efforts-fail/ar/1.

19. Jim Collins, *Great by Choice: Uncertainty, Chaos, and Luck—Why Some Thrive Despite Them All* (New York: HarperBusiness, 2011), Chapter 3.

20. "In Business, Simplicity Is Golden," *Forbes*, February 26, 2009, http://www.forbes.com/forbes/2009/0316/017_current_events.html.

21. Dwayne Spradlin, "Are You Solving the Right Problem?" *Harvard Business Review*, September 2012, http://hbr.org/2012/09/are-you-solving-the-right-problem/ar/1.

22. IBM, "Leading Through Connections: Highlights of the Global Chief Executive Officer Study" (Somers, NY: IBM Global Business Services, 2012), 5–7, http://public.dhe.ibm.com/common/ssi/ecm/en/gbe03486usen/GBE03486USEN.PDF.

23. Quoted in Jim Kling, "Tension in Teams," HBR Blog Network, January 14, 2009, http://

blogs.hbr.org/hmu/2009/01/tension-in-teams.html.

24. A. G. Lafley and Roger L. Martin, *Playing to Win: How Strategy Really Works* (Boston: Harvard Business Review Press, 2013), 47.

25. Collins, *Great by Choice*, Chapter 7.

26. Lafley and Martin, *Playing to Win*, 211.

ABOUT THE AUTHOR

Steve Graves is an organizational strategist, pragmatic theologian, and social capitalist.

As principal at Coaching by Cornerstone (coachingbycornerstone.com), he advises high- profile CEOs, business owners, and young entrepreneurs. He sits on a half dozen boards, holds degrees in multiple subjects, writes often, speaks occasionally, and has co-owned over a dozen businesses. He and his wife, Karen, have three adult children and live in Northwest Arkansas.

For more resources from KJK Inc. Publishing, go to stephenrgraves.com.